In *Freedom From Fear Forever*, Mark has captured principles which, when practiced, will help transform a life from worry and fear to positive and fruitful action, not only for the doers, but also for those who they most surely will affect.

> Swen Nater, UCLA, NBA, ABA
> Author of *You Have Not Taught Until They Have Learned*

A book that will change your life if you use it as it was designed. Read it as the story first, the second time as the workbook, seminar format. It's life changing information. I appreciate having the e-book option with my travel schedule.

> Dan Poynter - Author of over 30 books
> International Speaker and Publishing Consultant

Mark has combined his considerable talents as a coach with his in-depth understanding of human nature to create a compelling motivation that allows the reader to gain a serious insight into self awareness. A must read for those with an interest in perpetuating personal growth and developing an understanding of the lost art of life's golden rules.

> Karl Bruno, Director of Food & Beverage, W Hotels

Tremendous effort. Mark has another best seller on his hands. *Freedom From Fear Forever* will change your life. This book is a must read!

> Andy Fracica - York Brand Marketing Manager
> York Unitary Products Group

There are hundreds of inspirational books that don't inspire and thousands of self-help books that leave you with more questions than answers. Mark's latest book is head and shoulders above the pack when it comes to helping you with life's real challenges and opportunities. I highly recommend it. Read it and you will never be the same again.

> Tim Connor, CSP - Best se

D1115795

This book is at once inviting and a q irrefutable. For those of us with crazy schedules, this is good stuff.

> Dottie Gandy - Speaker and Best Selling
> Author of *30 Days to a Happy Employee*

Freedom

from

Fear

Forever

By Mark Matteson

**Executive
Books**

Freedom *from* Fear Forever

Published by
Executive Books
206 West Allen Street
Mechanicsburg, PA 17055
717-766-9499 800-233-2665
Fax 717-766-6565

www.executivebooks.com

ISBN-13: 978-0-937539-44-6
ISBN-10: 0-937539-44-9

LCCN: 2005926398

Printed in the United States of America

07 06 05   5 4 3 2 1

Layout by Kevin Thomas
Cover Design by David Marty
Illustrations by David Harrison

This book is dedicated to my wife, Debbie of 25 years. You deserve a medal for putting up with me all these years! To my boys, Colin, Evan and Larod, you are great teachers, thanks for all the lessons. Your children will be blessed with wonderful fathers.

Acknowledgements

We would like to thank the following people without their help, this book never would have happened:

Kevin Thomas, you are the kind of person I want to be when I grow up; Charlie Jones, for his able example and inspiration; Jason Liller, for his ongoing support and encouragement; David Harrison, for his artistic gifts - We all knew in 7th grade you had immense talent. To all my friends that so selflessly proofed and edited the manuscripts; Jim Norris, for your wisdom, honesty and kindness; Mike Murphy, for your belief in me and rapid response; Alex Carney, what can I say, buddy, you're the man; Matt Peterson, your focus and discipline is amazing; Doug Widenmann, for swinging open doors; Mickey Smith, for your curiosity and kindness; Andy Fracica, what can I say except thanks, man; Dan Poynter, for your selfless teaching and able example; Tim Connor, for being farther ahead on the track and slowing down to help me; Dotty Gandy, you go, girl; Major Guy Brillando (he trains F-16 fighter pilots, for crying out loud!); Bob Moawad, for a lifetime of coaching, inspiration and perhaps the most generous guy I know; David Marty, for your speed, kindness and skill; Dan Holohan, a twin son of a different mother; Lori Maycock, your accomplishments both personally and professionally are an inspiration to everyone you meet; Chuck Blouse, a raving fan in PA; Adams Hudson, the guy who has forgotten more about Marketing than I will ever know; Drew Cameron, thanks for spreading the word; David and Marty Indursky, for your friendship and trust; and to all the Len's in my life: Rod Hoover, Les Dicks, Bob Moawad, Charlie Jones, Ken Blanchard, Rick Busby, Randy Dec, Charlie Morgan, Wade Brewer, Chuck Orton, Dale Rossi, Jim Hussey, Jim Marsh, Ken Krell, Mark Sangerman, Alan Weiss, Andrew Bennett, Patricia Fripp, Ruth King, Swen Nater, Tom Piscitelli, what can I say, but thanks for your friendships, coaching and help.

If I left anyone out, please forgive me.

ACKNOWLEDGMENTS

Table of Contents

Preface

Many people from the four corners of the globe have told me via email, voice mail and in person that they are reading and re-reading "Freedom From Fear," carrying it around with them for reference. I appreciate this, and continue to be grateful for it. The reach of the book continues to astound me. It is all over the world and I stand in awe. Len continues to teach and make a difference in the world. I feel blessed to have been able to tell this story.

Early one morning, basking in the glow of a positive voice mail, an idea began to form in my mind: a companion, a workbook, a follow up to assist in making many of the simple principles live and breathe might be a good idea. It's what Len would want. This follow up, this companion, represents his secrets, his formulas, his disciplines in detail and exploring much further what made him tick and succeed. If Len were coaching you, these are things he would have you do and know more about. The following is a follow up to all the inquiries of Len, his ideas, practices and disciplines.

I discussed this idea with my dear friend and publisher, Charlie "Tremendous" Jones and his enthusiastic response was, "What a tremendous idea!" (I would expect nothing less from him, as his passion for life and people continues to astonish me.) It is our wish to provide more value to enhance the experience of Len's Lessons.

If you made the investment in this companion, it means you are serious about your own personal and professional development. I applaud your courage and efforts.

These questions, quotes and stories can have a profound effect upon your better future. For enlightened self interest reasons, let "Len's Last Lessons" change your life for good. He will coach you, guide you, and nudge you to become the very best you can be.

Here are some suggestions for getting the most out of this book. The great value of attending a seminar, listening to audio or reading a book is not what you read, rather it's what you THINK about that counts. In this book, there is a place to capture YOUR thoughts and feelings at the end of each chapter. Consider the following strategy for getting the most out of this book:

1. Read the book all the way through as a novel
2. Re-read each chapter slowly with a pen in hand underlining passages that stand out for you.
3. As you complete each chapter, write down your thoughts, feelings and action items.
4. If you want to assimilate the strategies and philosophies, teach the principles to someone else as soon as possible. It's called dual plane learning. It's the best way to take ownership of ideas.
5. Buy two copies and tear the chapters out of the book to carry with you for review at odd moments throughout the day.
6. Repetition is the mother of skill. Until you have read something at least seven times, you do not have ownership of it.
7. Give the book to someone else you care about. For how it will make you feel.

Most of us are operating on less than five percent of our potential. Like an iceberg, most of what we can do is below the surface, unseen, and unappreciated. Let's push more of that above the water line.

Experts say each of us has deep reservoirs of ability, even genius that we habitually fail to use. You are so much more than others or yourself know, understand or appreciate. It's time. Let's go!

Visit www.ffffbook.com for updates and tools for growth.

Freedom

from

Fear

FOREVER

Chapter One

"The Wedding"

It **was a simple wedding.** Len had just turned 21, his bride to be, 19. She was radiant. Her long auburn hair fell gently around her flowing white gown. Everyone said they were too young. Len and Cheryl knew differently. It was fate. They were meant to be together. They knew it from that first encounter.

They met in High School. Len was working for the school newspaper. He was assigned a project that required he interview students with a tape recorder. It was an old tape recorder he had borrowed from his father. She had looked longingly into his eyes as he asked the questions.

Love is a magic carpet ride, a dream, a long slow ride in the tunnel of love at the state fair. The first cut is always the deepest. Len was smitten, head over heels. Love is a drug. Most of us forget over time how overwhelming those first feelings of true love are.

Nothing is more powerful than Love. It is the strongest emotion a man ever knows. It unleashes creativity, creates drive and energy where none existed before. Len had dated other girls, but nothing could have prepared him for how she made him feel.

She gave him a reason to succeed. Pleasing her was his highest ambition, his only goal. It is how God meant things to be. After four years of dating, Len knew. It was right. He was ready. Len had taken a job selling projects for an Air Conditioning company. He showed up early and stayed late. He had big dreams. One day he would own the company. He had a 10-year plan. Salesman, Sales Manager, General Manager, Owner. The Service Business, that was the way of the future. He kept his dreams to himself.

The day of the wedding, Len's father took him to breakfast. As they finished their scrambled eggs and toast, his father slid a beautiful binder across the table. It was a leather bound book. Len looked surprised.

"Len," his father said in a warm tone, "What I am about to give you represents the things I feel are most important for you to remember as you start this new life. I hope you take the lessons to heart. They represent a lifetime of ideas, mistakes, lessons I have learned. My hope is you read them over and over again, make them your own. Then, as you experience new ideas, insights and lessons you can add to this organic document for your son or daughter. Only then will you appreciate this journey called life."

The brown leather was impressive, the binding cracked as he opened it.

In Shakespeare's classic play, HAMLET, there is a beautiful and bittersweet scene where Polonius is offering some fatherly wisdom to his 18 year old son, Laertes. It is that poignant moment in every father's life where he must see his son off to college, the military, or life. It's sad because, for all intents and purposes, it really feels like the last moment you have to tell your son all the things you wish you had, but either forgot or simply didn't make the time for. It is in that spirit I write this to you…

Polonius
The wind sits in the shoulder of your sail, and you are stayed for. There-my blessing with thee, and these few precepts in thy memory:

Look thou character.

Give thy thoughts neither tongue, nor any unproportioned thought his act.

Be thou familiar, but by no means vulgar.

Those friends thou hast, and their adoption tried, grapple them unto thy soul with hoops of steel, but do not dull thy palm with entertainment of each new-hatched, unfledged courage.

Beware of entrance to a quarrel; but being in, bear that the opposed may beware of thee.

Give every man thine ear, but few thy voice.

Take each man's censure, but reserve thy judgment.

Costly thy habit as thy purse can buy, but not expressed in fancy; rich, not gaudy, for the apparel oft proclaims the man, and they in France of the best rank and station are of a most select and generous chief in that.

Neither a borrower nor a lender be; for loan oft loses both itself and friend, and borrowing dulleth the edge of husbandry.

This above all else, to thine own self be true, and it must follow as the night the day, thou canst not then be false to any man.
Farewell. My blessing season this in thee!

Laertes
Most humbly do I take my leave, my lord.

Polonius
The time invites you. Go, your servants tend.

Len read it ever so slowly, like one might read poetry. Soaking it all in.

In his father's own hand, almost like calligraphy, it said:

A Letter to my son, "Lessons from my Life"

You will never become wealthy working for someone else. This country was made great by the risk takers, the small business man. The rich buy assets. The poor only have expenses. The middle class buy liabilities and think they are assets. Wealth is a person's ability to survive so many numbers of days forward. If I stopped working today, how long could I survive? Choose Wealth every day. It beats poverty. Spend less than you earn. Develop passive income to cover all your expenses. There is truly no limit to what can be achieved if you don't care who gets the credit on your team.

Update your goals every year on paper, preferably on your birthday. Show up early and stay late in all your endeavors. It's never crowded on the extra mile. Do what you love and forget what other people think. Find your bliss and follow it. Give yourself at least seven years to turn the corner. Stretch your comfort zones every day, something simple like eating left handed or driving a different way home or letting the waiter order your meal for you in a nice restaurant. If you can't change the little things, the big changes will be very difficult.

Read and write something every day, specifically in your journal. Plan your day on paper every day, even weekends. Simply write down the six most important things you need to do today. It is true, time is money. Under-Promise and Over-Deliver in all things, especially in business. Get in the habit of surprising people with more value by managing the customer's expectations. Follow hunches; write them down in your journal. You just never know.

It doesn't take any extra effort to be nice; in fact, it's easier.

It takes a conscious decision every day to be kind, helpful, gracious, accepting, patient, and caring. It takes a decision and action every day.

Every person has a story to tell. Your job is to listen until you get to hear it. When you dominate the listening, you will be welcome anywhere.

Say something nice behind someone's back every day...it will get back to them. If someone provides great service, do two things,

1. Leave a nice tip

2. Call their boss over and praise him or her.

No one likes to be "should" on. Regardless how immature or selfish their behavior might be, avoid offering free advice. It's neither free nor welcome.

If you want to influence others, try:

1. BEING the person you want them to be

2. Model the behavior you talk about

3. Tell stories about times you screwed up and what you learned

4. Borrow other people's stories to serve as warnings or examples

5. Praise the slightest progress in others

6. Affirm that they will do great things with sincerity and conviction, touching them on the shoulder while smiling.

Hug your kids every day. Read to your children from classic literature from age five until fifteen or until they tell you they don't want you to anymore.

Tell your children with sincerity and warmth as many times as possible: "You have accomplished far more than I ever did at 18 and will continue to do so in all your endeavors. Your future is so bright it burns my eyes to look at it." Treat everyone you care about as if it's the last time you will ever see them.

The quality of your relationships with others will match the quality of your life. Getting along with people is an art to be mastered for a lifetime. People who need love the most appear to deserve it the least. Call your mother once a week and tell her you love her. No matter how old you get, she still needs to know you are okay. The older I get the less I care about defending my position. I would rather be happy than right. Your children are flowers. If you neglect the garden, they will grow wild. Love is spelled TIME in the garden.

Tell your children, "No matter what happens, win or lose, I am always: ***1.** Proud as I can be of you.*
                        ***2.** Love you unconditionally."*

Other people will forget what you say and maybe even forget what you do; however, they will always remember how you made them feel. Forget getting even with someone or defending your position with someone who lacks social graces. It's a waste of time. Just pray for them instead.

Buy the best clothes you can afford, always. Take the time to shower, shave and look nice before you go out of the house. People WILL judge you in the first five seconds whether you believe it or not.

Ask the question, "How did you get started in your business?" to everyone you meet, and dominate the listening. Everyone loves to talk about themselves. Everyone has a story. Ask a successful person what their favorite book is. After you hear the title from more than one person, go buy it and read it! Read the New York Times Sunday Edition at least once a month. Invest a lazy Sunday morning and get through most of it. It doesn't get much better than that.

Write people "Thank You" notes as soon as possible. It's best the same day. If you don't, the inspiration will leave as fast as snow in Seattle.

Make or buy dinner for a friend that has just suffered a loss or has been injured. For how it will make you feel. Make friends with the janitor, busboy, baggage handler, shoeshine guy and cab drivers. They have their thumb on the pulse of society, but no one ever pays attention to them. Show them the same respect you would the CEO of a large company. Never criticize the competition. It's bad business.

Develop the habit of forgetting what you do for others and remembering what they do for you. You'll be a lot happier when you stop keeping score.

Always offer others a choice of yeses in all you do. We all like choices, especially if they are in our enlightened self-interest. Every deal you will ever make is negotiable, especially if you are willing to walk away or have cash. There is always another deal. Ask for what you want. Don't be shy. Unassertive people have skinny kids. Be bold but kind, persistent but empathic, assertive but courteous. Get good at understanding why people buy. What are their motives? Everyone is in sales; the only question is, 'How good are you at it?' We make a living by what we get. We make a life by what we give. It's easy to trust God when things are going well. The true test is: Do you trust him when it's not?

When it comes time to take the credit in a team effort, give it away to your teammates. When it comes time to take the blame, assume it all. That is real leadership. When someone says, "Trust me," don't! If it sounds too good to be true, it usually is. Say "please and thank you" as you look the person in the eye with the biggest smile you can muster. Good manners don't take much extra effort. If you can't remember someone's name, reach out your hand and say, "We've met before, my name is Len"...and then wait.

Remember people's names. Teddy Roosevelt memorized all 1000 Roughrider's names. It put him in the Whitehouse!

When you know you are wrong, admit it promptly and with sincerity. When you are right, remain silent. You will be the same person in five years save for two things, the books you read and the people you associate with. Choose both wisely and in accordance with your goals. Keep your discontents a secret. Nobody cares. ATTITUDE is more important than the past, than circumstances, than failures, than successes, than education, than money, than what other people think, say or do. It is more important than appearance, giftedness or skill.

Smashing the other fellow's furniture will never make mine look any better.

If you have no time for prayer and meditation, you will have lots of time for sickness and trouble. Act as though I was and I will be. GOD is ready the moment you are. Peace of mind first and all things will follow on that.

Face the facts candidly, only then you can change them. Peace of mind is the one thing that matters. There is absolutely nothing else in the world which is equal in value to it. Nothing else that life can offer is more important than that and yet it seems to be about the last thing that many people work for. Under any circumstances, you must keep your own thoughts poised, tolerant, and kindly. Remember the Golden Rule.

There is always tomorrow. Things have a way of looking different in the morning. Remember to ask: 'How important is this, really?'

Look for ways to praise...every day. Make a gratitude list when you are feeling down. Without love or a vision we perish. Make certain you always have both. Hoarding ideas or knowledge comes from a place of lack. Sharing ideas or time comes from a place of abundance. If you give away all you know, it forces you to replenish and learn. Somehow the more ideas you give away, the more come back to you. Keep reading more than anyone you know.

Len was overwhelmed. A tear began to well up. This was 55 years of wisdom. His father had put a great deal of time and effort into this gift.

"Dad," Len said holding back the tears, "Thank you."

His father smiled, appreciative of the fact it meant something to Len.

"It's just the foundation. You build a nice house on top of it. Add to it. Give it to your son or daughter. It's a legacy, a shade tree."

They sat silently for five minutes. The coffee was cold. It was time to get ready for the wedding.

Chapter Two

"Len's Last Lessons"

Most of the lessons learned from Len happened in coffee shops, on long walks, driving, via letters and emails. He was a wonderful teacher. The relationship was based on the fact that he was the coach, I was the player.

The meetings were 30 to 60 minutes in length. Much of my personal development (or as Len used to call it, "Self Betterment") came after he pointed me in the right direction and I ran with the ball.

I have attempted to gather up as much as I can remember or have captured in my own journals. Many other Len's have appeared in my life since his passing. I am grateful to all of them. The lines blur and I am certain I give Len much credit for things I learned from other teachers. (My apologies to those coaches.)

"Fear," Len said one day, "is described in Webster's Dictionary as 'Sudden attack, danger, peril, a feeling of anxiety caused by the presence of evil, danger or pain, real or perceived. A feeling of dread, uneasiness, doubt or disquiet."

He paused, looking up to collect his thoughts. "It's a feeling of intense worry, manifested by the individual. It's the opposite of hope, optimism, positive expectation and the feeling that everything will work out just fine.

It's something that begins in the mind and if nourished, affects our emotions and ultimately our actions and decisions. That's why we must talk them over with a trusted advisor, counselor or coach. It tends to significantly diminish its hold on us when we disclose it to someone we trust."

"Did you always have the confidence and abilities to change your direction or attitude?"

"Heavens no! All this was learned."

"From...?"

"Books, people, experience, observation, trial and error, a lifetime collection forged by fire in the real world. I am always looking to make new mistakes."

"As opposed to the same old ones?"

"Precisely!"

"It's Mental Management, Self Betterment, a commitment to a new way of life that was very different than the one I learned growing up. You see, most of the people I observed or was influenced by did not embrace the ideas I will share with you. The disciplines and habits were as foreign to me as the Greek language."

"So there is hope for me?"

"For all of us. Most people are paralyzed by fear. If we learn to overcome it, we take charge of our life and world."

He smiled as I took notes.

"Fear grows out of the things we think. Compassion grows out of the things we are and what lives in our hearts."

"Why have you invested so much time into me and my self betterment?"

"By sharing this with you, I get to hear it again. Teaching is Dual Plane Learning. When we know, we must teach. We learn it on a deeper level, a more permanent one. We can't change destination overnight, but we can change direction today!"

He handed me a page from his journal. It said:

Len's Lessons

OBSTACLES are what we see when we take our mind off the goal.

"Since you get more joy out of giving joy to others, you should put a good deal of thought into the happiness you are able to give. How can you increase your service to others?"

"Don't walk in front of me, I may not follow. Don't walk behind me, I may not lead. Just walk beside me and be my friend forever."

Albert Camus

Look for the causes of your success. If someone tells you that you were great, say, 'Thank you. Why do you say that?' and listen. Only then will we know the common denominators of success.

Joy and Self Respect are independent of environment. It comes from within. It comes from embracing a sense of purpose. It comes from believing the work you do has meaning; that you have worth."

-Dr. James Dobson

"I encourage you to listen to your own small, still voice. The greatest value of our time together will be what you think about afterward, what you write in your journal, what you remember, what you come up with on your own. I encourage you to write down your own thoughts and feelings after each meeting we have together. None of us is guaranteed tomorrow. My hope for you is you have freedom from fear forever!"

MY thoughts and feelings:

_____

_____

_____

_____

_____

_____

Chapter Three

"Hard Habits to Hide"

"**First we form habits**, then they form us," Len said. That really stuck with me.

He went on, I just let him, "Good habits are hard to form but easy to live with. Bad habits are easy to form and hard to live with!"

I loved the little quotes and aphorisms.

"What is a habit?" he asked me with a serious tone.

"Isn't it something you do so many times and so often it becomes easy, natural."

"Yes," he replied, "and free-flowing. Simply stated, it's a

behavior you consciously or unconsciously choose to do over and over again. If you persist in any behavior, it eventually becomes automatic. Negative habits generate negative outcomes. Positive habits generate positive outcomes."

I wrote like a first grader with a box of 64 Crayola's.

"Most experts will tell you it takes 21 to 35 days to form a new habit, positive or negative. I believe that's true. However, some habits have taken us twenty or thirty years to assimilate. These are going to take some time to change."

He waited to let me get caught up.

"When I first started in sales, I found out in my second year that spending more time with people who can and will buy was harder than I first imagined. Those people were harder to see, but easier to sell. They are the economic buyers. This group had the authority to say yes, and did. The feasibility buyers, on the other hand, were not in a position to say yes, but would have you believe they could. They were easier to see but harder to sell. Persistence and creativity were habits I had to adopt in order to succeed."

"To stimulate your imagination and get the juices flowing, here is a list of GOOD Habits. Circle the ones you might adopt," he said in a fatherly tone.

They include:

* Eating well
* Talking about your concerns with a friend
* Making a gratitude list
* Journaling
* Reading great books
* Yoga
* Swimming

* Sharpening your professional skills with classes or seminars
* Acquiring a mentor to assist you in a specific area
* Listening to educational tapes or CD's while you drive, workout or walk
* Writing down your WINS
* Playing with your kids
* Walking the dog or playing with your cat
* Meditation
* Prayer
* Developing a passionate hobby/avocation
* Attending church
* Listening actively to friends or associates
* Developing empathy
* Being honest with yourself and others
* Optimism
* Forgiveness

Now make your own list of GOOD habits that you are willing to adopt and to commit:

1. _____
2. _____
3. _____
4. _____
5. _____

As I wrote, he would read or write in his journal. The he asked me, "What bad habits are currently in the way of your better future?"

1. _____
2. _____
3. _____
4. _____
5. _____

"This sounds like a lifetime process. How often do you look at these things?"

Len paused and said firmly, "Every year on my birthday! It's a good habit, once a year. I have a friend who passionately believes in every six months. Whatever works for you. The only important thing is you decide that Self-Betterment will be a life-long process for you."

Len's Lessons

If you are in Sales, spend time with people who will buy. They are hard to see, but easy to sell.

People who are easy to see are hard to sell.

First we form habits, then they form us.

Take stock of your progress once a year, perhaps on your birthday.

MY thoughts and feelings:

_____

_____

_____

_____

_____

_____

Chapter Four

"The Way of Wonderful WINS"

Len said to me one day, **"A great habit to adopt is capturing your WINS!"**

"When you say wins, how do you mean?" I asked Len with some uncertainty.

"Do you remember The Two Questions?" he asked, with a tone that implied that I better have adopted that discipline.

"Yes," I said with confidence and pride. "Each night, before my kids go to sleep," I replied, "I sit on the edge of their bed and ask them two simple questions: 'What was the most fun you had today?' I listen, smile and echo an emotion like, 'So, you were proud of yourself?' Then ask, "What are you looking forward to tomorrow?"

"It's a simple process, isn't it?"

"Yes, and it only takes a few minutes! The effect has been dramatic and powerful for my boy's self-worth, confidence and self-esteem."

Len smiled, obviously glad I had learned that lesson. "It's really reflecting on a WIN."

He paused as if to find just the right thought and then continued,

"As we have discussed before, good habits are hard to form but easy to live with. Bad habits are easy to form and hard to live with. Worry is a bad habit. For years I unconsciously formed the bad habit of focusing on the negative aspects of my day, reliving it over and over again. Many of us fall into that same trap with our habits of thinking. A cycle of fear begins when we forget to capture the positive things that occur in our personal and professional life. Why is it we only remember the single gutter ball and forget the four strikes and three spares when we bowl? Focusing on a past loss, a setback, a criticism, a project that went over budget, a lost sale, is a matter of focus. Reflecting on past failures ensures poor future performance."

"So, by capturing the WINS, I consciously shift my mental and emotional focus on the things that feed my soul?" I asked.

"Exactly! You see, if we balance the losses with the WINS, we get a more accurate view of our abilities and potential. Most of us are doing much better than for which we give ourselves credit. When was the last time you sat down and reflected upon five things that went well from your past that makes you feel great, empowered and positive?"

"Never."

"Well, I would like you to list five WINS from your past that empower you when you reflect upon the impact the experience had on your life."

He handed me a piece of paper:

Gimme Five WINS, Man

1. _____
2. _____
3. _____
4. _____
5. _____

After finishing the exercise, I asked Len, "Don't Ship's Pilots keep a Captain's Log?" (I was remembering television's Captain Kirk.)

"Yes, they do. So why not keep a WINS Log? In its simplest terms, a WIN is anything positive that happens to you in your personal or professional life. Your daughter hits the winning shot in the big game, your son comes home with all A's and a B, you get that big promotion, you just closed the biggest sale of your life, your company had a banner year of profitability. Whatever feeds your soul and makes you feel great!"

"Got it."

Len smiled. He leaned forward and said, "Before any big meeting, proposal, presentation, I go back over positive feedback from past WINS. I can feel myself becoming more confident with each review. I allow the positive feelings to well up inside me.

I call this flipping back on a WIN and then with all those positive emotions whirling around inside me, I fast forward to the next presentation. It's like a magic potion. It fills me with positive expectations."

His eyes would light up when he talked about this, it was passion and enthusiasm.

"What would happen if you chose to capture and review past experiences just before a big sales presentation, project proposal, corporate meeting, speech or meeting?" Len asked.

"I would have more confidence?"

"Yes! Here are some additional things to consider:

Review your WINS prior to any important opportunity. Find a special place to record these WINS. I like to use my journal, but I started on a napkin.

Capture them as they happen. By reminding yourself of your past victories, it helps you identify with potential rather than your problems or setbacks. It enables you to act from a position of strength, power and confidence."

"That makes sense," I said with certainty.

"Our limits are self imposed. Our potential and possibilities are far greater than we have ever imagined. We are capable of far more than we ever imagined. Take a picture of your WIN, if possible. Pictures are worth a 1000 words! Create a picture of things from the past and for the future."

"Goals?" I asked.

"Yes," said Len. "By finding pictures of what you want, look at it each day, you will manifest those things into your life much quicker."

He smiled as I shook my head in amazement. He could tell I was loving all this learning.

"In my journals, I capture key points: date, time, person involved, place and a few key words." He showed me an entry.

August 8, 1994

Lake Chelan, WA

0630 Sunday

Daniel's 3 on 3 team won the "18 and under Basketball Championship" in Lake Chelan this weekend. The expression on his face told the whole story. The cheers from the crowd filled him with joy. I was so proud of him. He is making great progress. He is right on track.

"So," I paraphrased, "if I make entries each night before bed and review the day's success, I will feel differently about myself."

"Yes! Len affirmed. "You will feel more positive and upbeat. Your self-regard will improve and that will affect every aspect of your life. I now capture my WINS daily. It has changed my attitude, focus and self-worth. Remember, good habits are hard to form but easy to live with. Bad habits are easy to form and hard to live with."

Len's Lessons

What was the most fun you had today?

What are you looking forward to tomorrow?

In your journal, capture the date, time, day and location. It will give you perspective when you go back and re-read them in the future.

Take pictures of your WINS if you can. They are truly worth one-thousand words.

Ship's Pilots keep Logs, why not you?

MY thoughts and feelings:

_____

_____

_____

_____

_____

_____

_____

_____

_____

_____

_____

_____

Chapter Five

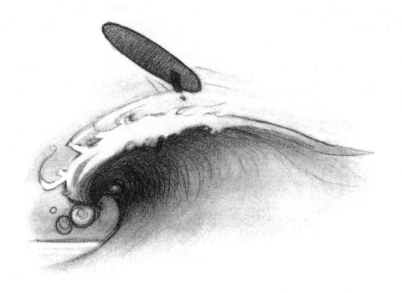

"successful states secured"

“**W**hat I am about to share with you,” Len said, “Is a secret to recapturing a state of mind that ensures your future success. **Not one person in 100 will engage in these disciplines.** Those that choose to will be absolutely astounded at the results.”

I leaned forward, pen in hand. I was ready. I would pay any price, change any behavior to achieve the things that had eluded me up to this point in my life.

“We talked about WINS. I now want to take you to another level of performance by borrowing that discipline and combining it with another that will increase your energy levels, increase your chance of success in any endeavor. Are you ready?”

His smile told me this was something special.

"Yes," I said, "let's do it. I'm ready!"

"As you know, I have been in sales for many years. Sales is really about managing activity and attitude. A positive attitude of mind is essential to success. Most sales people, once they attain that state of mind after sometimes weeks or months waiting to capture it, dilute it by not understanding its potential power."

I was taking notes as fast as he was speaking.

"These powerful, emotional states are elusive and temporal. When I first visited Honolulu, I was on the deck of a very nice hotel sipping a cup of coffee and watching the surfers early one morning. One fellow was obviously new to this challenging sport. He kept falling off his board over and over again. I admired his persistence. I watched him fall and get back on his board 10 times. Finally, he did it! He was up and surfed all the way into shore. He was ecstatic."

He paused and smiled. His face turned from fun loving to dead serious.

"Sales people work for weeks to finally make a sale. Then they dilute all that positive emotion by doing paper work, quitting for the day or having lunch. All that work is like struggling to get on the surf board only to jump off half way to shore."

I loved his stories. He always used metaphors.

"I will show you how to get and stay on your surf board quickly and consistently anytime you want. I want you to write down your five most significant WINS right now as fast as you can, in no particular order."

He handed me a piece of paper with the following written on it:

"Do you still have your five WINS in your journal?"

Pausing while he thumbed the pages, Len smiled and sipped his coffee.

"Here it is."

"Now, choose the most significant one, the one whereby when you reflect upon it, it brings back all those positive feelings. I like to call them 'Positive Butterflies.' Now, describe it in as much detail as you can."

Again, he handed me paper…

MY #1 WIN

_____

_____

_____

_____

"I like to call this "Rewinding." I grew up in the era of audio cassettes. In order to hear a favorite song again, we had to rewind the tape. Of course, that's not true today. That's all we are doing. By rewinding, we are re-visiting, recapturing a state of mind. Olympic athletes do this as part of their mental rehearsal. Many professional athletes have done it for years. It's one of the reasons they succeed."

"Almost like daydreaming or a fantasy?"

"Exactly!" Len exclaimed, obviously glad I was getting it.

"Now, before you have a big meeting, sales presentation, project or any important undertaking, REWIND. Then at the moment you have recaptured that State of Success, picture or imagine the future event in as much detail and imagery as you can. See the audience clapping, the prospect signing the agreement with a smile, whatever the desired outcome."

"So, it's a kind of flip back, flip up kind of thing."

"Precisely! You see, your subconscious stores all of your experiences, real or imagined, true or false. It cannot, it will not differentiate between actual or visualized moments. Every time you visualize a positive outcome, with positive emotions, it's worth sixty times the actual experience! Our brain is the most amazing computer of all, and the best part is it's programmable by us! A twelve year old child can do this, and some do. It's really Peak Performance Training of the most wonderful kind."

"How often should I do this," feeling a little overwhelmed by the information.

"Whenever you need to get back on track, whenever you are stuck, think of it as a Talisman. Do you know what that is?"

"No, I'm afraid not," I said a little embarrassed.

"A Talisman is a touchstone, a method and system that will work for each of us to counteract failure, inertia and discouragement. It's anything that which its presence exercises a remarkable or powerful influence on human feelings or actions.

You can't always change your destination overnight, but you can change your direction, the set of your sail."

Len paused for just a moment, like someone shifting gears to speed up.

"If I may mix my metaphors for a moment, if you choose to adopt this great habit, your surfing will improve and you will make more sales, achieve much more in your life due simply to successfully managing your states (of mind). "

Len's Lessons

Sales is about managing Activity and Attitude.

Stay on your surfboard and ride it to shore.

Use Positive Butterflies to your advantage. Leverage past success for the future.

Use one big WIN as leverage for the future.

After I make a sale, I need to suspend my desire to do paperwork, take a long lunch or go golfing. Instead, I need to make five or six more telephone calls, send out ten emails to prospects. Why? Because I am in a different emotional state, with more confidence, everything is different inside me.

MY thoughts and feelings:

_____

_____

_____

_____

_____

_____

Chapter Six

"Wondering about Worry"

"You wouldn't worry quite so much about what other people thought of you if you only realized how little time they actually did!"

"That little quote changed my life forever," Len said to me one day in a coffee shop. "It's funny how one little maxim, at just the right time, can stick. That quote came at a time when I most needed it from a mentor who simply was a much better mental manager than I was. Other people are caught up in their own life challenges and simply don't have time to worry about me and my problems. That is the objective reality of life."

I interrupted Len's train of thought to interject something a doctor had told me once. I had echoed concerns my friends had shoved down my throat about the amount of hours I was working. They had said to me, "You shouldn't be worried about that. It's not good for you."

The doctor's reply, "Worry affects the circulation, the heart, the glands, the whole nervous system. I have never known a man who died from overwork, but many who died from doubt and fear!"

Len smiled. "I concur," he continued. "Did you know that worry is interest you pay on trouble before it comes due?"

I grabbed my journal.

"Experts estimate that of all the things we worry about, forty percent will never happen, thirty percent are past and all the worry in the world cannot change them, twelve percent are needless worries about our health, ten percent are petty, miscellaneous worries, leaving only eight percent for things that legitimately deserve our concern, attention and thought. Eight percent!"

"If that's true, I have been wasting a lot of time and effort."

"Until we become good mental managers, that is true for all of us," Len replied.

"Years ago, I ran into an old girlfriend that I had not seen since college. I had always felt guilty about my behavior in that relationship. It had ended badly; I had been a jerk. I had carried all that guilt and shame around with me like Ebenezer Scrooge's business partner, Jacob Marley. Do you remember the scene from that classic Dickens tale? Jacob has all those chains and boxes around him. He shows up in Ebenezer's bedroom one night to warn him. At that moment, that's how I felt when I ran into her. I seized the opportunity to apologize to her. It was at least 12 years after the fact. She smiled and said simply, 'I really don't remember, but it was good to see you. Take care.'

She didn't remember? I had carried all that stuff around with me and she didn't remember? THAT, is the plain and simple truth. Other people move on with their lives. I need to as well."

"For every negative channel, there is a positive one, just like on your television set. Simply change the channel. Positive opposites!"

"Positive opposites?"

"Yes. Turn a negative into its opposite on paper.

Hate .... Love
Injury.. Forgiveness
Doubt.. Faith
Despair.. Hope
Darkness.. Light
Sadness.. Joy
Self Pity.. Service
Resentment....................................... Pardon."

Len smiled and left me to the first exercise.

"I want you to make a list of all the worries you have currently.
Put them on the list below."

1. _____

2. _____

3. _____

4. _____

5. _____

6. _____

7. _____

8. _____

9. _____

10. _____

"As you reflect upon the list, consider the following questions:

1. What is the one legitimate concern that deserves your attention?

_____

2. What CAN you do about it?

_____

3. What is out of your control?"

_____

Len's Lessons

You wouldn't worry quite so much about what other people think of you if you only realized how little time they did.

Worry is like negative goal setting.

Worry is interest you pay on trouble before it comes due.

Only 8% of our worries are worth our time and consideration.

MY thoughts and feelings:

_____

_____

_____

Chapter Seven

"Who were your Great Coaches from your past?"

"**H**ave you ever read 'The Odyssey' by Homer?

"No," I said a little embarrassed. The books this guy reads!

"In that story," Len responded, "is a character by the name of Mentor. He was the wise man of the village. He carried a large stick. People came to him for advice and counsel."

He paused, then said, "You will be the same person you are today except for two things, the people you associate with and the books you read," Len said to me. Of all the quotes from him, that was the most often repeated.

He continued, "Who are you hanging around and why? Is it okay? Choose your friends and mentors carefully. Our associations, the people who influence you, in a subtle but definite way, nudge you to your future. It's a powerful determinant as to where we end up."

Len had so much knowledge, the kind of information I never learned in school. I was grateful he made the time to teach me.

He continued, "I had a shop teacher that brought the very best out of me. I drew 23 mechanical drawings over Christmas break in 1971. Don't ask me why," Len said with a Mona Lisa smile emerging from his lips like a cat creeping up on a canary, "I just wanted to."

He took a sip of his coffee and looked off in the distance as if he were searching for an answer on the ceiling to help him continue.

"At the time, I couldn't tell you exactly what it was he did. He inspired me to do my very best. I wanted to please him, make him proud. I wanted to get an A+ in his class. In retrospect, every great teacher, coach and mentor shared the same qualities as that shop teacher in 8th grade."

I thought for a moment of the teachers and coaches I had that did the same thing for me. As if he were reading my mind, he said:

"Let's conduct a little exercise. Who were the great coaches, teachers, relatives and friends that positively impacted your life?"

He handed me a piece of paper and walked away. Just before he got to the door, he said, "I'll be back in 30 minutes. We'll go over your insights."

Below you will find a replica of the form Len had handed me. Invest 30 minutes to uncover your best coaches, teachers and mentors.

Let's Create a Timeline:

Jr. High School * =1==2=3======4==5==6===7===8= * Present
1970   2006

WHO?

1. (1970) The first mark in time was Bob Smith, my 8th grade Shop and Mechanical Drawing Teacher. I loved his class and did well....

2. (1974) The second mark was my Junior Year in High School, 1974, my German Teacher, Ms. Heinrich: "Ich spreche gans Deutsch und…"

3. (1975) Bob Mueller, a Motivational Speaker and Basketball Coach. I attended a two day seminar, then attended it again a year later…

4. (1982) Karl Linder, my first great boss. As Service Manager, he believed in me and gave me a job and a chance…

5. (1988) Greg Rogers, my first Great Sales Manager

6. (1993) Charlie Johanson, my publisher

7. (1997) Alan Wells, Consultant, Author, Speaker

8. (2006) Paul Meisner, Author, Speaker, Consultant

What qualities and characteristics did they possess?

What did they bring out in you?

_____

How did they do it?

_____

What are the causes of their success?

_____

"It was important for you to reflect upon your past," Len said with certainty.

Pausing for effect, he continued, "Now that you have taken a snapshot of your past, let's discuss the future. Based on your Goals and Objectives, WHO are five people you could meet with to learn more about the attitudes, skills, and knowledge you will need to achieve those goals and objectives?"

"Do you want me to list them now?" I asked.

"Yes," he said, because we all need guides on our journey through life. More than just one guide. As you think of the mentors, ask yourself why you think each of them can be of assistance."

He waited for me to finish writing.

"There are some questions to ask once you have your face-to-face opportunity with a Mentor:

* How is it you have succeeded in your field?

* How long did it take you?

* How long would it take you today?

* What has changed?

* Is there a system to what you do?

* What would you recommend I do to achieve that kind of success?

* What is the most important lesson you ever learned?"

* What books should I read?"

"I have never been exposed to this kind of knowledge," I thought to myself.

How fortunate I am...

While the emotion was strong and the questions fresh, I proceeded to ask Len the questions...

Len's Lessons

You will be the same person in five years with the exception of two things...the books you read and the people you associate with.

Who are you hanging around and why?

What are you reading and why?

Who were the great coaches from your past?

Who are five people you could talk to and learn from?

MY thoughts and feelings:

_____

_____

_____

_____

_____

_____

_____

_____

_____

_____

_____

_____

_____

_____

_____

_____

Chapter Eight

"The Wonder of WORDS"

"Did you ever give much thought to the power of the words you use?"** Len inquired one day as we were walking around a track. He called it multi-tasking. On Wednesdays, if I wanted to spend time with him, it had to be at 5:00 am at the local Community College.

Len had an extra-ordinary memory. He would cite poems and verses verbatim. He let one loose that morning:

Watch your thoughts, they become your words;

Watch your words, they become your actions;

Watch your actions, they become your habits;

Watch your habits, they become your character;

Watch your character, for it becomes your destiny.

It all starts with your thoughts.

I was sad I didn't have a pen and paper. I made a mental note to find that verse.

"Did you know we all talk to ourselves at about 800 words a minute, or 60,000 words a day!"

I thought to myself, where does he get this stuff?

"When my first mentor challenged me to begin to examine my self talk, it was difficult. I had to begin by listening to other people's self-talk. It was kind of fun at first. I would hear negative phrases, things like:
"I am at the end of my rope," or "My head is about to burst!" or "What's the matter with me anyway, how could I be so stupid?"

Now I was really sad we were not at the coffee shop.

"It was a real ear opener. After a few weeks of listening to other people's self-talk, a whole new world was opened up to me. It was as if I had learned a new language. In a way, I really had. It was the language of success and the language of failure. I eventually began to call this Inclusion and Exclusion."

"Exclusion?"

"We all use certain phrases or words that either empower us or hold us back. Negative words or exclusionary language sounds like this: 'I'll TRY and get that information to you.' Or, 'I would do that but THEY won't let me.' "

He paused to let me get caught up.

"Then there are the SHOULD-ERS!"

"SHOULD-ERS?"

"Oh, yes, they are the worst. They SHOULD on themselves and others all day long and aren't even aware of it. You know, 'I SHOULD start working out!' or 'I SHOULD start reading more!' "

"Those are the same people that offer unsolicited advice to others and can't seem to understand why they offend everyone they meet!" I offered.

"Exactly!" Len smiled.

He continued, "They go a few steps further, with exclusionary language like 'Swamped, Someday I'll, Problems, Can't, That drives me nuts'...the list goes on and on."

"Hey, wait a minute. I use some of those expressions and words!"

"I know. I have heard you," he said with a smile.

"So, how come you didn't correct me?" I asked.

"You weren't ready. I would have overwhelmed you and scared you off!"

"So, how do I change my language?"

"By being aware of your own self talk and identifying words that don't serve you well. Change the phrases into positive opposites."

There is a very simple prayer written by Reinhold Niehbuhr that does an amazing job of changing words and habits from positive to negative:

Grant me the serenity to accept the things I cannot change, the courage to change the things I can and the wisdom to know the difference.

"So you're suggesting I say that prayer every day?"

"It's what I do. That's a decision only you can make. It works for me. I had made myself a promise many years ago that from today forward, I would capture the words I hear myself saying that get in the way and find the opposite. From there it's as simple as forming a new habit. It worked for me. I found I was holding myself back unconsciously."

"What if you used new words, powerful words, words that empower you?"

Without waiting for me to respond, Len continued.

"I put those in the Inclusion category. Awesome, Beautiful, Colossal, Definitely, Ecstatic, Fantastic, Great, Hilarious, Intense, Killer, Loving, Magnanimous, Powerful, Resilient, Super, Terrific, Utterly Awesome, Wonderful."

"So, it's about monitoring the words I use for a month, perhaps even writing them down. Then, replacing them with more powerful and effective words?"

"Yes, simple, not easy. You can do it. I believe in you!" Len said, touching my shoulder as we parted. His words and smile left me feeling that I could change.

Len's Lessons

Watch your thoughts, they become your words;

Words become your actions, actions become your habits.

Listening to your own self talk is a real EAR opener....I need to write my thoughts and beliefs down and ask myself, is that belief going to take me where I want to go? Where did it come from? If it's not serving me, change or delete it.

Do you think we all need to stop SHOULDING on ourselves and others?

Grant me the serenity to accept the things I can't change and the courage to change the things I can.

What words would you eliminate from your vocabulary?

MY thoughts and feelings:

_____

_____

_____

_____

_____

_____

_____

_____

_____

Chapter Nine

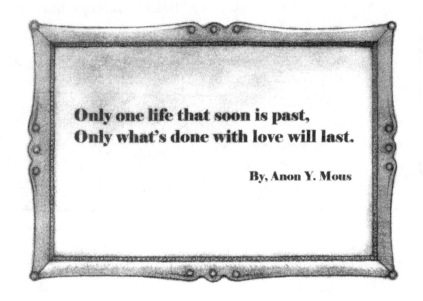

Only one life that soon is past,
Only what's done with love will last.

By, Anon Y. Mous

"Words on Your Wall"

Len knew a doctor that had a bathroom located next to his garage that was his. It was the only room his wife allowed him to decorate. **On it were plaques with inspiring quotes.** Here is a sampling of the poems, quotes and ideas that meant the most to him:

"Only one life that soon is past. Only what's done with LOVE will last."

Anonymous

"Not my will, but Thine be done." Luke 22:42

"SMILE and you are immediately happy." Henry Miller

EACH LIFE AFFECTS ANOTHER'S

"We may not always realize that everything we do
Affects not only our lives but touches others too,
For a little bit of thoughtfulness that shows you care,
Creates a ray of sunshine for both of you to share.
Yes, every time you offer someone a helping hand
Every time you have a kind and gentle word to give,
You help someone find beauty in this precious life we live.
For happiness brings happiness, and loving ways bring love, And
giving is the treasure that contentment is made of."

Amanda Bradley

"God grant me the serenity to accept the things I cannot change;
Courage to change the things I can,
And Wisdom to know the difference.
Taking this world as it is, not as I would have it.
Understanding that I can have peace of mind in this world;
And be supremely happy with Him in the next."

Reinhold Niebuhr

"There is wisdom:
In taking time to care,
In wanting to share,
In Grace and making amends,
In having and keeping good Friends."

Anonymous

"Everything wonderful begins with a dream."

Anonymous

"Though we travel the world over to find the beautiful,
We must carry it with us or we will find it not."

Ralph Waldo Emerson

"Hearts, like doors, will open with ease, to very, very little keys,
Like THANK YOU and IF YOU PLEASE."

Anonymous

"If a man is honest with others and with himself...
If he receives gratefully and gives quietly...
If he is gentle enough to feel and strong enough to show his feelings...
If he is slow to see the faults of others but quick to discover their goodness...
If he is cheerful in difficult times and modest in success...
If he does his best to be true to himself and his beliefs...
Then he is truly an admirable man."

Ralph Waldo Emerson

THE MAN WHO DARES
"The man who decides what he wants to achieve,
And works till his dreams all come true,
The man who will alter his course when he must,
And bravely begin something new,
The man who's determined to make his world better,
who's willing to learn and to lead,
The man who keeps trying and doing his best,
is the man who knows how to succeed."

WILL
"There is no chance, no destiny, no fate,
can circumvent or hinder or control
The firm resolve of a determined soul.
Gifts count for nothing, will alone is great;
All things give way before it, soon or late."

Ella Wheeler Wilcox

YOU MUST NOT QUIT
"When things go wrong as they sometimes will,
When the road you're trudging seems all uphill,
When the funds are low, and the debts are high,
When you want to smile but you have to sigh,
When care is pressing you down a bit,
Rest if you must, but don't you quit.

Life is strange with its twists and turns,
As everyone of us sometimes learns,
And many a failure was turned about,
When he might of won had he stuck it out.
Don't give up though the pace seems slow,
You may succeed with another blow.

Success is failure turned inside out,
The silver tint of clouds of doubt,
And you never can tell how close you are,
It may be near when it seems so far.
So stick in the fight when you are hardest hit,
It's when things seem worse,
That YOU MUST NOT QUIT."

Anonymous

"The voluntary path to cheerfulness, if our spontaneous cheerfulness be lost, is to sit up cheerfully, and act and speak as if cheerfulness were already there. To feel brave, act as if we were brave. Use all our will to that end and courage will very replace fear. If we act as if from some better feeling, some bad feeling soon folds its tent like an Arab and steals away."

William James

Len's Lessons
What words are on your wall?

MY thoughts and feelings:

_____

_____

_____

Chapter Ten

"Add Years to your Life and Life to your Years"

One of Len's friends told him a story once which he cherished.

As the story goes, he was repairing an ice machine in a very posh Senior Housing community. The lunch bell rang and in shuffled 35 women chasing one guy. His name was George. They ALL wanted him to sit at their table. As he was the only man in the room, he was one very popular fellow!

That experience began a chain reaction of thoughts. From that day forward, Len's friend began to study longevity. Why did some men live a long time and others did not? Was it diet? Exercise? Communication? Few people would argue the point that women, in the main, do a much better job of those three factors than men.

No, it wasn't that. It was purpose. Having meaning in your life. "Without a vision we perish," it says in the Old Testament.

Women never retire!

According to the actuary tables, 68% of American men in the U.S. are dead within 18 moths of retirement!

The famous men of history that lived a long time: painters, musicians, writers, actors, artists, all had one thing in common. They never retired. There was always one more song, movie, play, painting, or story.

George Bernard Shaw lived to be 92, Monet, 92, Mark Twain, 83, George Burns, 99, Bob Hope, 100. None of these men even considered retirement. They shared the following common denominators: First, They were doing what they loved. Next, they had goals, projects and objectives long into the future. They didn't care what others thought of them. They invested a lifetime in a passionate pursuit of their dreams. They never stopped learning about their chosen profession, they were serious students. They gave away what they knew to young people that shared a common pursuit."

"They had amazing ATTITUDES?" I asked, knowing the answer.

"Yes!"

Based on his tone of voice, I knew the good stuff was coming. I grabbed my journal and pen.

"The common denominators of their success: Their attitude, at the beginning of a difficult task, more than anything else, will manifest the results they seek. It's a mindset, a strong belief in their own abilities that will ensure their success."

"So, it's a decision?"

"Yes, on a daily basis," Len said with a smile. "Next, I must remember that I am a mirror. Whatever I give out is reflected back to me. My attitude toward others will always determine their attitude toward me! This is one of those ironclad laws."

I was writing as fast as I could.

"Before I can achieve anything I want in life, I must think, talk and act in all aspects of my life as would the person I wish to become. It's best if I have a written description of the kind of person I wish to become. I become what I think about."

He paused again to let me catch up. He was on a roll.

"The position one attains in business is a reflection of the attitude of the person. Most CEO's I know are there because of their attitudes. They do not have a good attitude because of their position. The right attitude always comes first, the position later. An attitude of other-centeredness, of service to others, of appreciation for other's strengths and skills will have a magic effect on other's self-worth. The deepest craving in the human condition is the need to be appreciated. A great habit to adopt is to catch people doing things right."

"This is common sense, isn't it?"

"More like uncommon sense. Most people have heard it, few apply it."

"For example, displacing the negative habits of blame, complain and explain with personal responsibility, gratitude and hard work is a habit. It's a hard habit to form, but an easy one to live with."

"Easier said than done?"

"Exactly! A variation of the Golden Rule is, treat everyone you meet as if they were the most important person on earth for several reasons: They are as far as they are concerned! It is how we should treat one another; it will become a habit."

"Len, I appreciate the time you are making."

"You are most welcome. I learn best when I teach. The next one is simple. Each of us loves to receive it." He paused, smiled.

"Smile. It takes 13 facial muscles to smile and 47 to frown. It's actually easier to smile. It's the universal language of success and joy."

Len practiced what he preached. He was always smiling. It was infectious.

"Learn the art of gratitude, acceptance and forgiveness. How important is it, really? Let the little things go that others do to and against you. You never know where they are at the moment. Become an optimist. Perpetual optimism is a force multiplier. Optimists live longer than pessimists do. It's a daily choice. It's how we see the world and how the world sees us."

My pen was ablaze, smoking. Len stopped. He got up and walked to the bathroom. My head was spinning. This was the good stuff.

"Did you ever notice how some people don't seem to be affected by all the negativity in the world?"

"Yes," I said with a hint of sadness. Thinking to myself, I thought of some organizations that seem to prosper in turbulent times. I finally said aloud, as if I was snapped out of a hypnotic trance, "How do they manage this magic act?"

"Well, I have been studying optimism, hope and peak performers with positive attitudes for almost 20 years. Here are some of the conclusions I have drawn," Len said with confidence and certainty:

"Human beings, by altering their inner attitudes of mind, can change their outer world in every aspect of their lives." He went on to say, "We need only act as if a thing were real and it will grow into such a connection with our lives, so knit with habit, that it will become real."

With a slight scowl, I replied, "So if I ACT AS IF, the feelings and results will follow?"

"Exactly!" Len said with a Cheshire cat smile.

Continuing on, he said, "I once knew a woman who increased sales in her company in one of the worst economic times the country had ever seen! Her solution was simple. She found and hired away the very best sales people from her competition, trained them like crazy and told them to DOUBLE THEIR ACTIVITY!" Guess what? It worked! It worked then, it will work now. She was an optimist! She believed in the best, expected the best and manifested it in her company. The power of belief is an amazing thing."

"I hate to keep asking dumb questions…"

"No such thing. Go ahead."

"So let me get this straight. What is INSIDE a person is far more important than anything going on outside a person?"

"Precisely!" He was grinning big now. "Manage your input by monitoring what you do, who you associate with, what you read and listen to."

I was writing like crazy.

Len's Lessons

Everything and everyone counts. There isn't anything that doesn't matter.

Act as if.

Do what you love.

Have goals long into the future.

Never stop learning about your field of interest.

Embrace a positive attitude daily.

Never retire.

MY thoughts and feelings:

_____

_____

_____

_____

_____

_____

_____

Chapter Eleven

"Attitude Adjusted"

"A **n attitude of hope and positive expectancy** is central to success. Maintaining an attitude of hope, backed with persistence and working smart with a focus on the needs of customers will always bear fruit," Len said one day on a long drive to hear a nationally known speaker. Len attended five or six seminars a year from the time he was 21 years old. He attributed that habit to much of his philosophy, ideas and success. He told me a story:

"An old man was sitting on the edge of town when a stranger with a frown and furrowed brow approached him. 'Say, old man, what kind of people live in this town?' asked the stranger. 'What kind of people lived in the town you left?' the wise man replied. 'Oh, they were mean, critical, negative and angry. I couldn't wait to leave!' said the stranger. 'That is exactly the kind of people you will find in this town. You might not be very happy here. I hear there is a wonderful town about 50 miles west of here that's just what you're looking for.' The grumpy stranger moved on without a word of thanks. About an hour later, another man walked up to the old man with a big smile on his face. 'Good afternoon, sir. Pardon me, but could you tell me what kind of people live in this town?' the enthusiastic young man asked. 'What kind of people lived in the last town you lived in?' the old man inquired. 'Oh, they were amazing, kind, generous, thoughtful, I hated to leave,' the young man replied warmly. 'You'll find the same kind of people in this town…welcome! I hope you stay a long time.' "

I really liked Len's stories. They always had a point.

He continued, "Did you ever see the movie 'Patch' Adams?"

"Wasn't he played by Robin Williams in the movie?"

"Yes," Len replied. "He has changed the face of medicine from a frown to a smile. In his biography, "Gesundheit," he is described by others as 'A Reminder.' He reminds people they need: To be listened to, given hope, joy, empathy, humor, fun, faith, love, intimacy, wisdom and wonder. We forget."

I was taking notes.

"My friend Doug is one of the funniest and most optimistic people I have ever met. Last I heard, he is 92 years young… Doug played Vaudeville. He wears a beret. He has a tremendous sense of humor. He is fond of saying, 'I am so old I don't even buy green bananas anymore!' He continues, 'I get out of bed, I put my feet on the floor, it's a good day, I am on this side of the grass.' Finally, 'Take it from me, don't worry about senility. When it hits you, you won't know it!' He is always smiling. It's a habit anyone can adopt."

"Doesn't that help in Sales, too, for making a good impression?" I asked.

"Absolutely! We buy from people we LIKE, TRUST, and KNOW ARE COMPETENT. Consider a little self deprecating humor. It disarms people and opens up their hearts and minds. We need to develop the ability to laugh, at ourselves and adverse circumstances that are out of our control. No matter how bad things get, the tide always comes back in, and when it does, all the boats in the harbor rise."

Len gave me a minute to get caught up. I glanced up from my notes as we drove, and interjected, "I read once that Tom Edison was so deaf at the age of 12 that he could not hear a bird sing. What to others seemed a poignant tragedy was to the Genius Inventor/Industrialist, a fortuitous break. Ambient noise was immaterial. He insisted that being deaf set him apart from the masses of men and gave him an excuse to turn away from tiresome social involvements, making him a far more productive THINKER."

"So you're reading biographies of great men?" Len inquired.

"Yes," I replied with a grin. "I got that from you. Did you know Edison learned to ask the question of himself, 'How do you know it's bad?' We can always turn lemons into lemonade with a little creativity and effort."

Len interjected, "So much of it depends upon the attitude we choose to embrace. It's not what happens, it's how we respond. Optimists live longer than pessimists do, and they have a better time along the way!"

"It's what optimists DO and BELIEVE that separate them from their pessimistic counterparts: "The defining characteristic of pessimists is that they believe bad events will last a long time, will undermine everything they do, and are their own fault. Optimists, who are confronted with the same hard knocks, think about misfortune in the opposite way. They tend to believe defeat is just a temporary setback, of which its causes are confined to this one case, and are unfazed by defeat. They perceive it as a challenge and try harder the next time. They must believe that they CAN change it in the future."

"So what we have talked about before, fanning the flames of success by capturing their WINS, contributes to that?" I asked.

"Yes. You see, when something good happens in your life, a big sale, your son or daughter succeeds in sports or music, it's so important to write it down, to capture it!"

"That ties into controlling my self-talk and means I need to stop 'Shoulding' on myself," I stated, paraphrasing Len's message.

"Yes. You see, if we change the destructive things we say to ourselves when we experience setbacks, everything changes. *Learned Optimism* is just that, learned. If we aspire to succeed in turbulent times, we must learn we CAN take control of our life and improve, change, grow, evolve, and become. Expect to succeed, choose to change, be accountable and give up blame."

"So if I am hearing you right, optimism is a daily choice, sadly, so is pessimism."

"Absolutely! As Jackson Browne sang years ago, 'No matter how far I run, I never seem to get away from me.'"

Len's Lessons

What kind of people live in your town?

We all choose to live in the town we are in.

An attitude of hope and positive expectancy is central to success.

Maintain a sense of humor, even under the most adverse circumstances.

No matter how bad things get, the tide always comes back in, and when it does, all the boats in the harbor rise.

We can always turn lemons into lemonade with a little creativity and effort.

Learned Optimism is just that, learned.

Where is your focus? Positive or negative?

MY thoughts and feelings:

_____

_____

_____

_____

_____

_____

_____

_____

_____

_____

Chapter Twelve

"A Gaggle of Goals"

"WE BECOME WHAT WE THINK ABOUT," Len said with authority.

I nodded in agreement.

"How many of us actually understand and apply it? What do YOU want to accomplish this year? How badly do you want to achieve it? Do you have your goals written down and do you look at them every day?"

"So, you are saying if it's worth achieving, it's worth writing down?"

"Yes. Here are some basic fundamentals to review and apply to achieve all you want in life."

Len handed me a quote from Thomas Carlyle,

"A person with a clear purpose will make progress on even the roughest road. A person with no purpose will make no progress even on the smoothest road."

I read the quote. I inserted it in my journal.

Len continued, "Successful people think about their goals most of the time. As a result, they are continually moving toward their goals and their goals are continually moving toward them. It's the law of focus. Whatever you think about most of the time increases in your life. If you are visualizing, thinking on, writing about, and reflecting upon your goals, they will manifest themselves into your life...there is no way they cannot."

"How long have you been writing your goals down?"

"Since I was 14 years old."

"I'm getting such a late start."

"No, you weren't ready. You are now. Let's keep going. Here are some thoughts on goal achievement. Decide exactly what you want in one key area of your life. Write down your goals clearly and specifically. Something amazing happens between your head and your hand when you put your goals on paper."

"What about timelines?" I asked.

"Set a deadline for each goal. Set sub-deadlines if a goal is big enough. (i.e., break it down into quarters, months, weeks, days, number of telephone calls, etc.)"

"Then make a list in your planner, journal, PC or Palm Pilot of everything you can think of that you will need to do to achieve each goal. As you think of new ideas, add them to your list until it is complete."

This was great stuff. This was clearly the 'How to' I had been looking for.

"Organize your list into a plan of action. Determine what you will do first, second and so on. Decide what is more important and what is less important. Prioritize."

Len gave me a few minutes to get caught up.

"Take some action immediately. Do something today to move you closer to your goals! I like to make a list of 10 Goals to accomplish for the year. Once I capture them, I rewrite them in affirmation format. Make sure they include the four "P's": Personal, Positive, Present Tense, Powerful."

He smiled. He could tell I was grateful for this specific information. My face lit up like 4th of July fireworks.

Now, which 'ONE GOAL' on this list, if you were to achieve it, would have the greatest impact on your life? That is your #1 Goal! Circle it and rewrite it onto a 3 x 5 card. Review your 3 x 5 card, at least three times a day, reading the card aloud with emotion and passion. Let the joy of achievement sink in!"

Keep your goal in your journal and look at it at least five times each day. From time to time, thoughts, hunches, insights, ideas will emerge. Capture them. From now on, think and talk to yourself about that goal all the time."

"You had mentioned reading books in alignment with my goals?" I asked. I could feel my confidence and enthusiasm growing.

"Yes, read about your goal topic at least 15 to 20 minutes each day. Furthermore, make a list of people who could serve as mentors to assist you. Email, call or write to at least three of them for advice on books, seminars, people, strategies."

"Write your #1 Goal on a 3 x 5 card and keep it on your dash board. Have a list of reasons why you want that goal in your life! Reasons are the motivating forces that drive us. Desire improves our circumstances. Given a sufficient quantity and quality of reasons, we can always find a way to scale the highest peak, or swim the deepest ocean. Knowing the 'How to' is not as vital as knowing clearly the 'Why to.' Reasons attract solutions. You don't get the answers to do well until you get the reasons."

My head was spinning. I was so excited, I could hardly sit still. Len continued, "Life has a mysterious way of hiding all the answers for doing well and turning them loose only to people who have enough reasons. What are your reasons? Personal reasons, Family reasons, Benevolent reasons, Economic reasons, Spiritual reasons. The better your list of reasons, the better your chances of succeeding in any endeavor!"

"Can you give an example of what the written goal might sound like?"

Len handed me a piece of paper. He was always prepared.

"This was some of the information I used to share with my sales reps when I was a sales manager."

SAMPLE Language of well written Sales GOALS

* "I am a relentless marketing man (or woman)!"

* "I love what I do and it shows!"

* "I have a passion for prospecting and gaining referrals!"

* "I am at ease in front of people!"

* "My enthusiasm pulls people into the sale."

* "I was born for this work!"

* "I am passionate about my life's work."

* "I close my sales with the utmost sincerity and conviction!"

* "I believe I am making a difference in my customer's lives."

* "I am an excellent Active Listener!"

* "I summarize my customer's core concerns, feelings and issues."

* "My prospects feel understood, respected and appreciated."

* "I am prepared in all sales situations."

* "I am a voracious reader. I watch video, read books and listen to audios/cd's to improve."

* "I love to learn. I am a serious student of sales."

After I had read through his sample goals, Len continued to end our session with a bang:

"To be successful you must have a plan. A plan means goals, a track to run on, and a system of priorities. Do first things first. You must have goals and deadlines. Set goals big enough to get excited about and deadlines to make you run. One isn't much good without the other, but together they can be tremendous. Sales is a great example. We need a track to run on. Set a plan big enough to get excited about, and break it into timing, then into ideas, then into three proposals a week. Would you like to sell a million dollars of your product or service as your goal?

You can't? Too big? Break it apart into little pieces. Separate it into months…then weeks…then into simple sales packages…three a week. Now it can be done. You have a track to run on. Make it big enough to be exciting, then break it down into little pieces so it's do-able. Organize your time so you put in a full day's work."

I had read about Michael Jordan. I handed Len a page from my Journal.

I ask questions, I read, I listen…I'm not afraid to ask anybody anything if I don't know. Why should I be afraid? I'm trying to get somewhere. Help me, give me direction. Nothing wrong with that. Step by step, I can't see any other way of accomplishing anything.

Len smiled. He took the page and thanked me.

Then he handed me a number of typed pages.

"Here is your homework for the weekend. The following exercise will add years to your life and life to your years. Furthermore, they will help you clarify your objectives, give your life a sense of purpose and light your fire in a big way."

My Lifetime Goal List

List as many Lifetime Goals as time allows…in no particular order:

HAVE:

1. _____

2. _____

3. _____

4. _____

5. _____

6. _____

7. _____

8. _____

9. _____

10. _____

SEE:

1. _____
2. _____
3. _____
4. _____
5. _____
6. _____
7. _____
8. _____
9. _____
10. _____

DO:

1. _____
2. _____
3. _____
4. _____
5. _____
6. _____
7. _____
8. _____
9. _____
10. _____

BECOME:

1. _____
2. _____
3. _____
4. _____
5. _____
6. _____
7. _____
8. _____
9. _____
10. _____

SHARE:

1. _____
2. _____
3. _____
4. _____
5. _____
6. _____
7. _____
8. _____
9. _____
10. _____

"Now, go back over each goal and ask yourself, is it a 1-year, 5-year, 10-year or 20-year Goal? Write a 1, 5, 10, or 20 in the left hand margin.

Pay attention to the 1-year goals. We will come back to those.

Now take a break and go get yourself a cup of coffee or tea.

Now it's time to narrow the focus. Review your Lifetime goal list and choose ten, one year goals."

This Year's Top Ten Goal List

"Rewrite your 1-year goals below and then prioritize the list in the left hand margin.

If you could only accomplish one thing this year, which one would you want to achieve first? That one is #1.

Of the nine remaining goals, if you could only accomplish one goal, which one would it be? That one is #2, and so on down the list.

1. _____
2. _____
3. _____
4. _____
5. _____
6. _____
7. _____
8. _____
9. _____
10. _____

Now, re-write your "Number One Goal" using the Four P's of Goal Achievement onto a 3 x 5 card. The Four P's are:
1. P = Positive
2. P = Present tense
3. P = Powerful
4. P = Personal

Now, list five reasons WHY you want to achieve this goal. W.I.I.F.M.= What's In It For Me? Reasons will pull you to the future!

What might be some of the barriers?

_____

_____

_____

What are the solutions for those challenges?

_____

_____

_____

Now read your goal card aloud 5 times a day for 30 days. If anything positive happens, do it again for another 30 days. Write it out in your journal every morning. Visualize achieving it and how it will feel. Like Aladdin's Lamp, ideas, people, insights will materialize in the 60 days to help you along the way. It is truly magical. Try it for 60 days…"

Len's Lessons

We become what we think about.

If it's worth achieving, it's worth writing down.

A person with a clear purpose will make progress on even the roughest road. A person with no purpose will make no progress even on the smoothest road.

Decide exactly what you want in one key area of your life. Write down your goals clearly and specifically. Something amazing happens between your head and your hand when you put your goals on paper.

Reasons are the motivating forces that drive us.

Keep your goal in your journal and look at it at least five times each day. From time to time, thoughts, hunches, insights, ideas will emerge. Capture them. From now on, think and talk to yourself about that goal all the time.

I ask questions, I read, I listen...I'm not afraid to ask anybody anything if I don't know. Why should I be afraid? I'm trying to get somewhere. Help me, give me direction. Nothing wrong with that. Step by step, I can't see any other way of accomplishing anything.

MY thoughts and feelings:

_____

_____

_____

_____

_____

_____

Chapter Thirteen

"Efficiency Vs. Effectiveness"

"**If you lean your ladder against the wrong building**, it doesn't matter how fast you go up and down the ladder," Len exclaimed, as we began our next meeting.

"So you are going to teach me how to lean my ladder against the right building?" I asked.

"Yes. You did the homework on your goals. The next challenge you will be faced with is what to do with each day.

Let me tell you a story."

I smiled and settled in for the day's lesson.

"It seems one night a farmer had a dream. In his dream he had

seen a pot of gold in an unused portion of his land. The west 10 acres was where he had stumbled across the treasure. So vivid and real was the vision, and so great were the benefits in the dream, he could not stop thinking about it. The following morning he enthusiastically got up an hour early, and did this every day for 30 days, to dig in a different part of the property. At the end of the month he had dug up the entire 10 acres and alas, there was no gold to be found. Frustrated, he sat down to ponder what had gone wrong. Unable to resolve his dilemma, he did the only thing he knew how to do, that was farm. He planted seeds in the tilled soil. Come harvest time in the fall, he enjoyed his first bumper crop. With the additional revenue, he was able to make the much needed repairs to his equipment, pay off his loans and put some money into his savings for the first time in years."

Satisfied with himself, he sat back, took a sip of his coffee and waited.

"So, the moral is, like the farmer, if I carve out some extra time, perhaps even get up an hour early to plan my day, I can enjoy a bumper crop?"

"By Jove, I think He's got it!"

Len handed me another page.

Len's Daily Planning Process

1. __ Carve out 15-20 minutes at night or in the morning (whenever you are the most effective, alert and energized.)

2. __ Review unfinished action items from yesterday, the monthly action item list and your #1 goal. What can you do over the next few days to move toward that goal?

3. __ List the six most important things to do today.

4. __ Prioritize in order of importance (if you were going out of town for 30-days, which one would you do first?)

5. __ Estimate how long you think the action item will take in brackets, i.e. (1 hr.)

6. __ Review notes from yesterday. What did you learn?

7. __ Write out your #1 Goal 15x, say it aloud 50x or Visualize 2x a day.

8. __ Write down any thoughts, ideas or insights that come to you and list them in tomorrow's action item list.

Len's Lessons

If you lean your ladder against the wrong building, it doesn't matter how fast you go up and down it. It's the wrong building.

Plan your day every day.

What are the six most important things I need to do today?

MY thoughts and feelings:

_____

_____

_____

_____

_____

_____

Chapter Fourteen

"Oh yes, one more thing!"

"**Why set and achieve goals?**" I asked Len one day.

His answer surprised me. "For how they will make us feel about ourselves and who we must become in order to achieve them," he said with a smile.

When Len told me that, it came screaming through my filter system like a baby's cry to a new mother. It never dawned on me before that day, a different reason to set and achieve goals.

He went on to explain, "When we set a big goal for ourselves, we go through four distinct phases. I like to call them the Four A's:

AUDACIOUS, ATTAINABLE, ACHIEVABLE, AUTOMATIC."

He handed me a piece of paper.

AUDACIOUS

The goal seems so far out of reach, it's almost laughable. The first time I wrote down a huge goal that stretched my boundaries of comfort and sanity, I looked around hoping no one would see it for fear of what they would say. You know, "Who do YOU think you are?" "What makes you think YOU can achieve anything like THAT!??" I am certain now one of those voices was coming from me!

ATTAINABLE

"Maybe I can do this thing," we begin to think to ourselves. We gather glimpses of inspiration, moments of clarity, a modicum of expectancy, whereby we begin to form a new belief. It is very much like the first time you didn't fall for more than five seconds when you tried to ride that dreaded two-wheeler as a kid. HOPE.

ACHIEVABLE

Now it's within the realm of possibility. IF I stay on this path, it's really going to happen! Momentum, excitement, enthusiasm, energy, eustress (that is, a positive expectancy of the future, like how we feel the day before we go on vacation!) The feeling energizes us, keeps us up late, working and looking forward to tomorrow.

AUTOMATIC

Free flowing, natural, easy, an over learned skill like tying your shoe or driving well with one finger! We have turned it over to automatic, subconscious activity without giving it any real thought. Like a golf handicap in single digits. IF you have a lousy front nine and shoot a 45, your mind will correct for the error and your self-image takes over with self talk like, "That's not like me," or "This can't continue, I am better than this." What happens next is automatic, you correct for the error. You birdie the next three holes, one or two putt and chip like crazy…bingo, a 29 on the back nine for a remarkable 74! That's our belief system at work. It's true in commission sales, sports or any other endeavor whereby we see ourselves differently than our current reality sees.

It never ceased to amaze me, Len and his wellspring of information.

After I had read the page, Len continued, "When we set goals, just reading them every day even many times a day is not enough! We must act! A goal without action is just a wish. We are deluding ourselves. Here are some actions that will speed up the achievement process. Invest in a journal to capture all the learning. This is where all the good stuff goes. Ask five people who have done what you want to do and been where you want to go a few questions:

1. What five *books* would you recommend I read?

2. What *seminars or workshops* should I attend?

3. What *magazines or periodicals* could I subscribe to that might help me learn more on the subject?

4. Which *films, videos or documentaries* could I watch?

5. What else should I know? If you were starting over, knowing what you know now, what would *YOU do differently?*"

"How long did it take you to gather all this information?" I asked in amazement.

"A lifetime," he said with a smile. He continued, as a man late for a flight at the airport.

"All this data is collected and archived in your journal. You can also turn the goal into a question and ask, "How can I reach my goal of $100,000 earned this next year?" and then sit and think for 15-

20 minutes each morning or evening. 30 days of this simple discipline will yield ideas you cannot imagine. You will be amazed that the ideas came from your own mind. Most of them will not be any good, but a few will be amazing."

"Doesn't all this take time and effort?" I asked, like a junior high school kid fearing the quantum leap to high school.

"Yes. But it's so worth the effort. What's the cost of not doing it? The great writer, George Bernard Shaw said to a reporter near the end of his life, in summarizing his extraordinary success as a writer, "I have become rich and famous thinking a couple of times a week!"

"Make up your mind. Do one thing or the other. Stick to your choice.
Never tell people about the fine thing you are about to do. Wait until you have done it. Talking about your plans before they have actually materialized is the surest way to destroy them. Under any circumstances you must keep your own thought poised, tolerant, and kindly."

"So, you are saying, make up your mind and just do it...silently."

"Yes...it's that simple, just not easy."

Simple, not easy, rang in my ears as I walked away.

"Why set and achieve goals?" I asked Len one day. His answer surprised me. "For how they will make us feel about ourselves and who we must become in order to achieve them."

Len's Lessons

Challenging and Big Goals follow a distinct pattern in our minds,
AUDACIOUS, ATTAINABLE, ACHIEVABLE, AUTOMATIC.

Invest in a journal to capture all the learning. This is where all the good stuff goes.

Turn your #1 goal into a question and ask, "How can I reach my goal?"

I have become rich and famous by thinking a couple of times a week.
George Bernard Shaw

Simple, not easy.

MY thoughts and feelings:

_____

_____

_____

_____

_____

_____

_____

_____

_____

_____

Chapter Fifteen

"The Value of VALUES"

"Why do we always meet at Starbucks?" I asked Len one day.

"It's the third place."

"The third place?" I asked completely clueless as to what he meant.

Len leaned forward, "It's not home and it's not work. It's the third place.

It's warm, restful, and comfortable. I always feel pampered, special, relaxed, at home without being there. THAT is what Starbucks sells. By the way, they are very successful financially with very little turnover for the retail industry. Do you know why?"

I shook my head.

"I was ordering a cup of my favorite coffee at my local Starbucks when I spotted "The Starbucks Mission Statement" hanging conspicuously on the wall at the point of purchase. Here is what it said (paraphrased):

MISSION STATEMENT

Maintain uncompromising principles.

Use our principles (Values) in making decisions.

Treat each other with respect and dignity.

Embrace diversity.

High standards of excellence to all aspects of business.

Satisfied customers all of the time.

Contribute to community and environment.

Profitability is essential to success.

"As I copied this information down in my journal, it became clear to me as I was writing that this ubiquitous billion-dollar coffee company does an outstanding job of living their values. Their people have been trained to live this creed and walk the talk. Not only are these sound and profitable principles by which to live your business life, they make good sense."

Len was on a roll.

"The organizations that soar are the ones that create great WORDS ON THE WALL, then work like crazy to live them every day. Repetition is the mother of skill. They make the language simple and easy to understand."

"Like FEDEX'S, "Absolutely, Positively Overnight!" or MICROSOFT'S "A Computer on Every Desk, Worldwide," I said with confidence.

"Yes! It's okay to change it as your business changes and grows. Look at FEDEX'S now: "The World, On Time." MICROSOFT has evolved to "Where do you want to go today?"

"What are your values?" Len asked me.

"I never really thought about it," I said, a little embarrassed.

"A mentor of mine asked me to make a list one day of all things I value most in life. After I was done with my list, he said something that hit me in the face like a two-by-four. He said, 'Show me your check book and day planner and I will tell you what you value.' "

"In other words, how I spend my time and money tells me and the world what is important to me?"

"Exactly!" "You see," he continued, "Values are the core beliefs that rudder your life. They define the very essence of your personhood. We get in touch with them by asking ourselves some important questions, like what am I willing to stand up for? Or what would I lay down my life for? What would I want my children to emulate?"

Len handed me a piece of paper.

What are my governing values?

1. _____

2. _____

3. _____

4. _____

5. _____

It was clear I had more homework. These questions, these exercises, were forcing me to think about things I never learned in school.

"I will answer these questions. Can we meet at Starbucks again next week?"

Len smiled. "Fair enough."

Len's Lessons

What is most important to me?

What am I willing to stand up for?

What am I willing to die for?

What would I want my children to emulate?

Show me your check book and day planner and I will tell you what your values are!

Starbucks has found a way to live their values.

MY thoughts and feelings:

_____

_____

_____

_____

_____

_____

_____

_____

_____

_____

_____

_____

_____

_____

_____

_____

_____

Chapter Sixteen

"Turning the Corner"

I rarely saw Len get upset or angry. I asked him about this one day on a long drive to the ocean. We were attending a seminar on "Self Respect," an intense, two-day seminar put on by a famous author.

"How do you keep your cool, Len?" I asked.

"I didn't always have a cool head and a warm heart. I had to undo a lot of old beliefs and habits. My transformation began with a story, one that really stuck with me. I'd like to tell it to you. It makes a great point."

"By all means, please."

"Genghis Kahn was a great King and fierce warrior. One

97

August morning he rode into the wood to enjoy a day's sport of hunting with his best friend and constant companion, his hawk. In those days, hawks were trained to hunt. They would fly high above the forest to spot opportunities. It had been a long and unfruitful day of hunting.

The King was very thirsty, but that time of year, the stream had dried up. Water was scarce. Finally, the King spotted a rock with water barely dripping from it seven feet high. He took out his cup and waited almost an hour for the cup to fill. As he brought it to his lips to drink, his hawk swooped down and knocked it from his hands. Confused and still thirsty, he waited a half an hour and with the cup half full, slowly brought it to his mouth. Again, his pet hawk swooped down and knocked it from his hands. Now the King was angry. His thirst had clouded his judgment. His third attempt was a copy of the first two. On his fourth attempt, now almost four hours after he had found the dripping rock, he drew his sword as he brought the cup to his lips. The Hawk was successful knocking the cup out of his hand for the fourth time, but as his winged friend flew upward, the King struck him with his sword and the Hawk fell quickly and began to slowly die at his feet.

Looking for his cup, he spotted it at the top of the rock, the source of the water. He climbed up and retrieved the cup for his fifth attempt. What he saw in the pool of water turned his blood cold. A dead snake of the most poisonous kind lay dead in the pool. He forgot his thirst. Had he drank the water from the cup, he would have most certainly died a painful death. As he buried his best friend that day, he made himself a promise, NEVER DO ANY-THING IN ANGER."

He looked straight ahead as he drove. He continued, "The turning point came for me one day when I backhanded my 14 year old son in front of the family. Everyone was stunned, including me."

His voice began to tremble. This was a painful story from his past.

"I broke down and cried. My wife said, 'You need to deal with this problem, it's getting worse!' My oldest son had gone to his room. I knocked on the door and asked permission to come in. He was sitting on his bed. I begged his forgiveness and made him a promise. 'Do you understand the difference between an apology and an amend?' I asked him. 'No', he said without looking me in the eye.

'An apology,' I explained, 'has no accountability and no change in behavior attached to it. They are just words. You see, an amend has an apology and a corresponding change in behavior.' I made an amend that day. I promised him I would change. I also said, 'I don't expect you to believe me right now. You WILL see a change in my behavior in the future. Please forgive me, son.' "

I was too shocked to say anything. I just listened as he had for me so many times. He seemed to appreciate that, and continued.

"True to my word," Len said with a most serious tone, "I went to work on that defect of my character, that bad habit that had crept into my life, like a thief in the night, wanting to steal the greatest possession I own, my family's peace of mind and security."

His voice trembled a bit as he continued.

"I attended several workshops on anger and read at least 10 books on the subject. For me, I discovered, it was about a loss of control. As he was flapping his wings of independence, that is adolescence, I was afraid. Fearful I would lose the little boy I loved so much. I was learning to let go. It was about learning to pick my battles with him and letting him win the little ones. It was about understanding the little annoyances that I had allowed to pile up each day, week and month. The fellow that cut me off on the freeway, the rude clerk at the retail store, the selfish neighbor with the barking dog, all the little things left unresolved."

"The collective weight, I was to learn of life's little peccadilloes, left untreated, and unforgiven were brought home to infect my family like a horrible flu. I had to learn to capture those little injustices as they occurred and accept or forgive as the situation dictated. It meant becoming a great mental manager 24/7/365 and leaving those people and their offending behavior out there, in the world. Most people are afraid, and that fear drives out impatient, inconsiderate, angry, selfish behavior. They are afraid they will not get what they want, or lose what they have. We are all that way from time to time. I learned to forgive, accept and move on in real time."

"How?" I asked.

"By writing them down in my journal as they came up. By saying a little prayer for them at that moment. By learning the principle of Displacement. By being aware. By engaging in the opposite behavior (Resentment replaced with Forgiveness). And by showing the same level of tolerance I might show a three year old child. You see, we are little children at times, me most of all. It meant growing up. It meant taking the low road, the path less traveled."

This was intense. It was a side and a level of honesty I had never heard from Len. This made him so human. I could feel his pain. My respect for him increased dramatically.

"For me," Len continued, "I go through a specific process. First resentment, then resistance and finally, revenge. It's an ugly place to go. I use up so much energy. Maintaining all that is exhausting."

"Can you walk me through that?" I asked.

"Certainly. Say a stranger cuts you off on the freeway, what do you do?"

"I honk and usually shake my fist!"

"Right, then you have a full fledged resentment. From there, you progress to resistance. Fight or flight. That's how most of us resist. It's really an attempt to control the situation. Whatever we resist, persists!"

I was nodding and taking notes.

"Finally, you want to even the score. Have you ever sped up and given the guy half a peace sign or tried to get in front of him?"

I laughed aloud. "Half a peace sign?" Shaking my head, I admitted, "Yes, more than once I'm afraid."

"Me too, for a long time. Then one day I realized, I was letting other people rent space in my brain. I was giving up my power to strangers. What I had to do was to grow thicker skin, colder blood and learn to let things go. The problem is most of the things I let go of have scratch marks on them."

"A surrender of sorts?"

"Exactly! We all reap what we sow. What goes around comes around. Birds always come home to roost."

Len and his aphorisms. Maxims that sound like contemporary proverbs.

"So, what is the answer?"

"Glad you asked. The secret was I had to become someone that reacts the opposite way than my instincts tell me to. I had to embrace forgiveness, surrender, compassion, acceptance, empathy. We all need to become 'Maniacal Givers.' Prayer works well. It sounds crazy, but it is really displacement."

"Displacement?"

"Putting rocks in a bucket full of water eventually displaces the water in it. By the time the bucket is full of rocks, most of the water is gone. That's what I had to learn how to do."

I found a little bit of prose I put on my dashboard for that first year that really helped.

Anyway

People are unreasonable, illogical and self-centered, love em anyway!

If you do good, people may accuse you of ulterior motives, do good anyway!

If you are successful, you may win false friends and true enemies, succeed anyway!

The good you do today may be forgotten tomorrow, do good anyway!

Honesty and frankness may make you vulnerable, be honest and frank anyway!

People favor the underdogs but only follow the top dogs, fight for the underdogs anyway!

What you spend time building may be destroyed overnight, build anyway!

People really need help but may attack you if you try and help them, help them anyway!

Give the world the best you've got and if you get kicked in the teeth, give the world the best you've got anyway!

People who need love the most appear to deserve it the least, give them love anyway!

Anonymous

"So, how long did it take you to overcome this challenge?"

"About a year. Some things take longer than others. I had spent a lifetime developing the bad habits, it would take a while to learn new skills and take them to the application level."

People from your past and present that you RESENT:

_____

_____

_____

_____

_____

_____

"After the list is complete, the next step is to forgive the people on your list."

"What if I don't feel like it?" I asked with a defiant tone in my voice.

"I understand that. I really do. For me, I found anyone I wasn't willing to forgive was like driving with my brakes on. I had to pray for them until I could forgive them. You see, resentment hurts me, not the person I resent."

"So I should set a goal to overcome this challenge?"

"Yes," Len said with a sad look on his face. "Then follow the same format I have for years,"

Len handed me a form:

Seven Simple Steps To Personal Change

1. With pen and paper, honestly recognize and courageously admit a challenge currently exists for you.

2. Write out the challenge on paper...Define precisely what it will cost you not to change..."A Pain Inventory" (10 to 20 REASONS.)

3. Write out a "Positive Opposite" onto a 3 x 5 card in a one-sentence description defining the new behavior as if it were true at this moment...NOW.

4. Ensure that your new written personal Belief is:
a) Positive
b) Present Tense
c) Personal
d) Powerful And Emotion Filled

5. List all the REASONS why it would be personally profitable for you to change at this time..."A Pleasure Inventory" (10 to 50 REASONS.)

6. Make a decision to read this description aloud 3 to 5 times a day and take consistent action for 21 days...a kind of test.

7. Reward yourself in some meaningful way for sticking to your decision. Continue to learn more about your new area of interest. Become an expert. Increase your awareness. Associate massive amounts of pleasure to this new behavior and objective. Whatever behavior is rewarded is repeated.

I knew over the next few weeks, I had real homework. This was the heart of "self-betterment."

Len's Lessons

Face your problems and act.

The difference between an amend and an apology is a change in future behavior.

We lack the means to change because we are afraid. Face your fears and the death of fear is certain.

Whatever we resist persists.

What goes around comes around. We reap what we sow. It's the law of cause and effect.

Displacement means putting something constructive and positive in place of something destructive and negative.

Some changes take longer than others.

What are your reasons to change?

MY thoughts and feelings:

_____

_____

_____

_____

_____

_____

Chapter Seventeen

"Till Death Do They Part"

When I said my marriage vows, I do not remember hearing, "Till something better comes along" or "Till you meet someone else" or "Till you just get tired of her annoying little habits." It says "Till Death Do You Part."

It really is true, women are from Venus and men are from Mars. It took me 20 years to finally begin to understand what women want. I spent the first 10 years of my marriage trying to figure out what I (men) wanted.

As I walked in the Starbucks, I held the door open for her. My first thought was I would lose my place in line by being nice. She turned to the right as if feigning looking at cups to give me a chance to get in line ahead of her. It was a little thing, but a big thing to me. She was thoughtful, empathic, kind. She was 20 years old. She was about 5'7", blonde hair, slightly curly and long. Her blue eyes were piercing and stood out against her fair skin and blond locks. She had an air about her, an attitude.

Our paths crossed again on the way out. "You first," I said, motioning with my hand. "Can I have the next dance?" she said with confidence and ever so slight sarcasm. She had a sense of humor.

I had grabbed my journal and was reviewing my notes and preparing for a meeting with Len. She, too, had a journal. She sat beside me at the next table. It turns out her name was Nellie. She was a student and worked part time. She asked what I did. The conversation blossomed and before I knew it, I was sharing many of the principles Len had taught me.

She was taking notes in her journal. After about 30 minutes, she had taken five pages of notes and was clearly assimilating the philosophy. I couldn't help it, I said with a smile, "Now my fee." She froze. "For my time and knowledge…you know, this mini-seminar." She wasn't sure what to think. Silence. "Here is the deal. You can't tell anyone I helped you." I paused for effect. "And, you have to help someone else down the road. It might be next year or 10 years from now…deal?"

She looked at my outstretched palm. "Deal!" she said with a big smile. The sigh of relief sounded like air leaking out of a tire through the service valve.

Now I know how Len feels. This is great.

Shortly after we struck our bargain, her fiancé came in. His name was Roger. He was tall, 6'-3", slender build, wearing a black and white baseball shirt with no logo. His jeans were faded, they hung on his waist low and loose. His thick brown hair was long and in a pony tail. He had three days growth on his face, his beard somewhat incomplete, like a painting that is only 75% finished. They were going to hear a famous author speak on relationships. That is where the conversation went.

"You have been married for a long time to the same woman, right?" Nellie asked already knowing the answer to the question. "Yes," I said, anticipating his next question. "What advice can you offer us?"

"I can only share mistakes I have made and things I have learned the hard way."

"That would be great," Roger said, with enthusiasm as he leaned forward.

"Well," I said with a tone of authority, feeling a little like King Solomon must have felt on his throne.

"There are three things I never heard before I got married. If I did hear them, they were gone quickly." They both leaned a little closer.

"I call them 3-C's. Communication, Cooperation and Compromise."

Nellie was writing it down. So this is how Len feels when I am taking notes.

"Your ability and willingness to talk and listen, always taking turns in the process. You see, men process in advance and then talk. It doesn't take much time. Women, on the other hand, process while they talk and it often takes 10 times longer but is no less important. Just a different style."

I could see this was news to Roger but not to Nellie. She nodded in agreement.

"Women see the inside of their house as an extension of their personality. How it looks, smells, feels are vital to them. For men, it's a place to kick off their shoes, watch the ballgame or movie, relax, read or veg. How it looks, smells, or feels is not as important. Understanding this simple clash in values helps in cooperation and compromise."

"The outside is more important to me," Roger said with confidence.

"Yes," I said. "That has been my experience as well."

"Marriage is like a song that is playing with no lyrics. You write the words as you go along. Pretty soon you have a whole first album. All I can do is share some song writing tips that worked well for me."

"She will want you to listen to her the same way and at the same depth that her best girlfriend does. She will have that expectation. Most men lack the desire or skills to listen that actively or at that level. The big challenge is managing expectations that each of you will have for one another. How the money will be used, where you will go on vacation, how many children will you have, the list goes on and on. That is why I go back to the 3-C's."

"Communication, Cooperation and Compromise?" she echoed.

"Yes."

As they left the coffee shop, I felt invigorated. I had helped this young couple, their lives so full of promise, dreams, excitement and hope. I remembered that time in my life as a newlywed couple. It is a time of positive expectancy.

I wished them well and watched them as they walked out. I hope they keep working on their marriage through all the winters that will most certainly arise. Financial winters, Health winters,

Relationship winters. Till death do they part.

You can't tell anyone I helped you.

You must help someone else down the road.

Len's Lessons

Communication, Cooperation and Compromise.

Women see the inside of the house as an extension of their personality, Men see it as a place to relax.

Marriage is like a song that is playing with no lyrics. We write the words as we go along.

Women are smarter than men. The difference between men and government savings bonds? Bonds mature!

MY thoughts and feelings:

_____

_____

_____

_____

_____

_____

_____

_____

Chapter Eighteen

"No Name?"

Len **was a very successful businessman.** At the heart of his success was his unique ability to remember people's names. It was uncanny. He wasn't always like that.

Len told me a story about a pastor that had a notorious reputation for forgetting people's names. As his congregation grew larger, the problem became worse. Finally, out of love, his assistants enrolled him in an adult education workshop designed to "Win Friends and Influence People." After many weeks of study, he called a meeting and enthusiastically announced the results. "I am happy to announce that I have dramatically improved my ability to remember names! That was time and money well spent. I feel so strongly, I have enrolled all of you in the DAVE Carnegie class!":)

As I listened to him, I reflected. When I was a kid, I had a terrible time remembering people's names. I've pondered long and hard as to why. Maybe it was that I never took the time to really listen. Maybe it was because I was always in a rush to get somewhere. Maybe it was my father telling the story of how bad HE was at names as a star athlete at his high school. Regardless, if you told me your name, it was gone from my memory as fast as a snowflake melts on the hood of a warm car in the dead of winter.

"My pastor friend developed the ultimate memory system. He has over 6000 names memorized!!

How? Why? "Simple," he said to me one morning over breakfast. "It requires becoming other-centered. That is to say, you have got to care more than most people are willing to. People don't care how much you know until they know how much you care."

"What are the reasons to invest the time and energy in learning this new skill?"

"Well, you will win new friends quickly and easily, and add luster and fun to all social situations and contacts. You will move ahead in business rapidly by developing a reputation for being caring and kind."

I was writing like crazy.

"You will sell more of your product or service."

"Isn't this the practice of the Golden Rule by Doing unto Others?"

"Exactly! You will truly esteem others and they will enjoy being around you. Finally, you will be in a very elite and small group of people with this skill. You will separate yourself from most of the other people in your peer group or organization."

"Okay," I said interrupting him, "How?

I wanted to learn Len's secret.

He said to me, "Just remember I.R.A. The I stands for Impression. I have trained myself to really listen when being introduced to anyone."

"So, it's really concentrating on getting the name right?"

"Exactly! If you don't hear the name clearly, ask them to repeat it. Try saying, 'I'm sorry, I didn't hear that clearly. Your name again was?' I've never had anyone get upset at that question."

"What if you are still unclear?"

"I ask them to spell it. Unless their name is John or Bill, they won't mind or be offended. I've found that most people are flattered that you asked."

"What's next?" I asked with pen in hand.

"R stands for Repetition. It's been said, 'Repetition is the mother of skill.' You can remember almost anything if you repeat it often enough. When introduced, repeat his/her name immediately ALOUD. Say, 'How do you do Mary, it's nice to meet you.' "

"What about using Mary's name several times in conversation?"

"Be careful not to overdo it," Len said. "Perhaps two or three times in a five minute conversation is plenty. However, you can repeat their name silently to yourself four or five times while listening."

"Is that it?"

Pausing for a moment, he continued, "If you are going to be with people with whom you don't normally spend large amounts of time, review their names, REFRESH your memory prior to an event. Dwight D. Eisenhower did this prior to inspecting his troops training in England during WWII. Ike would study the list of officers' names he was scheduled to meet that day."

"Wasn't he elected President after the War?"

"Very good. Yes, he was."

"What about the A?"

"A stands for Association. Consider forming an Association with the name. rhyme, repetition, silliness, exaggeration, similar names, or mind pictures."

"So, let me get this right."

Len was smiling at my paraphrase, something else he had taught me.

"The key acronym is I.R.A.—Impression, Repetition and Association. Easy to remember, and what a difference it will make to how you are perceived by your customers. Remember, a person's name to him/her is the sweetest sound in any language; it is their badge of individuality, as unique to them as their fingerprint. History is replete with examples of man's vanity around his name."

"Here comes a story," I thought to myself.

"In an effort to leave a legacy, James B. Duke, the cigarette king, offered to give tiny Trinity College in Durham, N.C. $40 million dollars if the college would change its name to Duke University!"

Len would occasionally let a stream or flow of information. It was a cloudburst of knowledge, like a spring shower.

He ended with a postscript. "If you invest the time and energy in this new skill, the results for you both personally and professionally will be out of all proportion to the effort. It will add quality and a subtle positive aspect to all your relationships. And besides, you won't have to spend weeks in that DAVE Carnegie class!"

Len's Lessons

Remembering people's names means becoming "Other-Centered."

The sweetest sound in any language for anyone you meet is the sound of that person's name.

I.R.A. means Impression, Repetition, Association.

Teddy Roosevelt and Dwight Eisenhower credited remembering people's names as one of the keys to their being elected to the presidency.

People will forget what you say, they might even forget what you do, but they will always remember how you made them feel. Remembering someone's name will make them feel special, important and that they matter.

MY thoughts and feelings:

_____

_____

_____

_____

_____

Chapter Nineteen

"Power of Public Praise"

Len's wife, Cheryl, told me one day, he always took an employee leaving very personally. It occurred to him one day, **"Why not ask them before they leave why they are leaving."** After a while, a list of the most common reasons began to emerge. He soon found out the reasons for departure were poor compensation, limited authority, personality conflicts, lack of appreciation, respect or understanding."

Len always said, "You can get great results from employees and make them feel valued so that they WANT TO do their best work on a daily basis, to consistently act in the best interest of the organization. You can get great results by focusing more on how you treat them."

He kept something in his wallet. It was his five great ways to boost loyalty, productivity and reduce turnover: Personal Heartfelt Thanks, Written Thanks In A Note, Promotion for Performance, Public Praise, and Morale Building Meetings.

Len realized that the Words and Phrases he habitually used were a big part of making people feel worthy and good about themselves, along with the simple habit of using the employee's name. He had four simple phrases he used consistently. He had them taped on the inside of his desk drawer in his office. It said: "I am glad you are here." "We are lucky to have you." "Thanks for all your hard work on finishing the XYZ project under budget and on time!" "You did a great job on this report, this sale, or this installation."

He liked abbreviations and acronyms. He used to say S.S.S.P.P.P. It meant praise should be Soon, Sincere, Specific, Personal, Positive and as Proactive as possible."

Cheryl paused for a moment to reflect.

"He found a way to make it a habit, a natural part of his daily routine. One manager friend of Len's began each day with five coins in his pocket. Each time he praised an employee with positive feedback, he transferred a coin to the other pocket. His goal every day was five coins transferred. Within a few weeks, he had formed a new habit."

She smiled as I pulled out my journal and began to take notes.

" 'The message you want to send,' he used to say, is: 'I saw what you did (others don't know what you see), I appreciate it (place value on the behavior or achievement), Here's why it's important (always provide a context), Here's how it makes me feel (give an emotional charge.)' "

Cheryl obviously knew as much or more than Len! She continued,

"The act of delivering simple, direct praise for a job well done is so easy to do; yet so many managers do not do it. Make the extra effort to appreciate employees, and they'll reciprocate in a thousand ways. If you don't, someone else will!"

She handed me a piece of paper.

What is Being Rewarded?

---

12 Effective Organizational Rewards:

1. Praise – Sincere, Soon, Specific, Personal, Positive, Proactive.

2. Time Off – Half days, full days, three-day weekends.

3. Recognition – High fives in the hallway, handwritten notes, pictures of employees' families, name and picture in the company newsletter.

4. Prizes – Movie tickets, dinner coupons, funny money.

5. Awards – Employee of the Month, The Extra-Mile Award, etc.

6. Money – Pay bonuses based on Gross Profit.

7. New Title – Chief Lizard Wrangler, VP of Customer Delight!

8. Favorite or Exciting Work – Internal Surveys asking your employees what they love to do, or how to make work more fun.

9. Advancement – Provide Peak Performers new responsibilities.

10. Personal Growth – Reward Peak Performers with extra Training, Education opportunities.

11. Freedom – Work one day of the week at home, flextime, three-day weekends, and no time clocks.

12. Fun – Christmas, Hanukah, and 4th of July parties. Birthday cakes/cards delivered on-site by the CEO, CFO, Service Manager, or Supervisor.

"Len understands what people really want," she summarized. "You will keep your best people, lower turnover costs and increase morale, productivity and profits."

My head was spinning. I had just received another huge lesson.

Len's Lessons

S.S.S.P.P.P means Sincere, Soon, Specific, Personal, Positive, Proactive.

I am glad you are here!

Thanks for all your hard work on the XYZ project.

You did a great job on this installation. It was on time and under budget!

If you are a manager, put five coins in your pocket every morning. Invest them in the power of praise.

Consider time off or flexible scheduling as an employee reward.

MY thoughts and feelings:

_____

_____

_____

_____

_____

_____

Chapter Twenty

"Dealing with Difficult People"

I was complaining to Len one day about a situation that I had handled poorly. **A customer had called and was unhappy.** I became defensive and he ultimately took his business elsewhere. It was not the first time this had happened. I was frustrated and embarrassed.

Len listened and smiled. He then tore a page from his journal and handed me the blank piece of paper.

"Write this down," he said, "I'll go slowly."

His well was deep. It seemed to me there was no topic he did not have a story for, no problem for which he did not have an answer. I started writing:

"Let me introduce you to: **L.E.S.T.E.R.**

It stands for:

Listen actively and with intention…
Echo an emotion
Sympathize or Empathize
Thank the associate for the opportunity to grow
Evaluate your options
Respond and follow through."

"I will let you catch up." He sipped his coffee.

"How do you know someone is actively listening to you?" Len asked softly.

"They make eye contact."

"Good. What else?"

"They lean forward, sometimes they smile or say 'uh-huh'. Little cues like that."

"Excellent. So, you can tell if they are genuinely interested by their body language."

"Exactly, like you do most of the time, Len. I have admired your listening skills since the first time we met. It's disarming, comforting, engaging. I have noticed people enjoy being around you, but they're not sure why."

"Oh, my secret's out. Be careful. If you make this a habit, things will never be the same. Everything will change: your bank account, your relationships with others, your awareness and knowledge."

"The E stands for Echo the Emotions you hear. This is very powerful. What emotions will you see and hear when someone is upset?"

"Anger, frustration, sadness, worry, and grief."

"Very good. You left one out."

"Fear?"

"Yes, fear." He leaned forward. "Fear we will lose what we have or not get what we want. It's a self centered emotion. It's very subjective. It's a habit. No one is without problems, but it is how we respond to those problems that separate us from the herd. Most people invest huge amounts of time worrying about their problems."

"You told me this, I wrote it down. If I remember right, we spend 40% of our time worrying about things that will never happen; 30% worrying about things that are over and past, 12% on needless worries about our health, 10% on petty miscellaneous worries and 8% on legitimate worries."

"Bingo! That means 92% of the time the average person worries takes up valuable time that could be spent in other ways, more productive ways!"

"The opportunity cost is enormous, isn't it?"

"Absolutely. It causes ulcers, headaches, nausea and anguish, and for what? It's so futile. It's like working hard sitting in a rocking chair."

"The S stand for Sympathy vs. Empathy. Do you know what sympathy sounds like?"

"Sure," I replied.

"That's too bad," "I'm so sorry that happened."

"Yes," Len said. "There is a time for that. There is also a time for Empathy. That's walking a mile in someone else's shoes. Having been where the other person has been, you can affirm their pain because it was first person for you in the past."

"What about the T? Thanking them?"

"It doesn't seem to fit, but it really does. When you thank a person for their honest feedback, it sends several messages."

"Like 'I can take it', or 'I'm glad you had the courage to speak up and tell me the truth?' I asked."

"Yes. Most people get defensive in a situation like that. They are taken aback when they hear your gratitude," Len said.

"I have been on the receiving end of that strategy with the manager of a hotel. He completely disarmed me."

"It's very effective," Len affirmed.

"The E is Evaluate your options. Something needs to change, people or process. The idea is to make new mistakes…"

"Not the same old ones?" I paraphrased.

"Exactly!" Len exclaimed.

"R is for Respond and follow through. Let them know what actions you took. It will go a long way in restoring the business or relationship. Remember, people will forget what you say, forget what you do, but always remember how you made them feel."

Len was the best teacher I had ever met. He combined his experiences with great storytelling and illustrations.

L.E.S.T.E.R. means:

Listen actively
Echo emotions
Sympathize or empathize
Thank others for feedback
Evaluate your options for change
Respond and follow through

Len's Lessons

People will forget what you say, forget what you do, but always remember how you made them feel.

Everyone from eight to eighty-eight craves three things from you: Appreciation, Respect and Understanding!

Just by actively listening to someone you can change their day, their week, their month, their year and their life.

An angry customer is like a whistling tea kettle. As you walk through this process with them, the water drops in temperature with each letter. By the time you get to Thanking the Customer, you can sip the tea.

MY thoughts and feelings:

_____

_____

_____

_____

_____

Chapter Twenty-One

"Mulling over Meditation"

One day I walked into the coffee shop at 5:30 am to find Len sitting **peacefully in a chair with his eyes closed.** He was the only person in the place. Not wanting to interrupt him, I bought a cup of coffee.

I sat down next to him and waited. Five minutes later, his eyes opened, he saw me and smiled. "Thank you for waiting."

When he was grateful, his eyes sparkled. There was a twinkle, a light that emanated from him. It was tangible.

Before I could ask, sensing my question, he said, "Have you ever meditated?"

"No," I replied, "at least not that I am aware of."

"Would you like to learn?"

"If it gives me what you have right now, then yes."

"Are you willing to trust me?

"Of course," I said, a little surprised by the question.

"This prayer comes from St. Francis of Assisi. He was born in 1182 and died in 1226. In the short time he lived, he lived as a shining example of service to others. Let's use his prayer. Close your eyes. Begin to breathe slowly. Breathe in for four seconds, hold for four seconds, exhale for four seconds. Do that four times. 4 x 3 is 12. 12 x 4 is 48. It's less than one minute. It's the best way of getting yourself centered."

There was silence while the master taught the student.

"Now, I want you to listen to the words I am about to say. Let the words soak in."

He paused, as if to let me get ready.

"Please Father,

Make me an instrument of your peace.
Where there is hatred, let me sow love;
Where there is injury, forgiveness;
Where there is doubt, faith;
Where there is despair, hope;
Where there is darkness, light;
Where there is sadness, joy.

Grant that I may not so much seek to be consoled as to console,

To be understood, as to understand,
To be loved, as to love;
For it is in giving, we receive,
It is in forgiving, we are forgiven,
It is in the dying of self, that we are born to eternal life.
Amen. Thank you, Father."

With my eyes closed, he continued.

"Now, just sit and wait. Wait for the insights, the ideas, the aha's that come from the silence, from the gap. When they do come, pay attention. Write them down in your journal. They come from another source, from God, from a higher power, from beyond, from time and space, from the infinite. It is only in the silence you will hear the things that will help you to go to the next level. At the next level, you will find joy, peace of mind, happiness, and abundance."

We sat in silence for five minutes. As I sat there, a couple of people came to mind, people that could use my help. It was hard. I wasn't used to sitting still. I had too much energy.

"A difficult discipline, isn't it?"

"Yes." He constantly paraphrased my thoughts and feelings. He always knew.

"Fifteen to twenty minutes a day is all you need to change your life. In thirty days, you have formed a good habit. One that will fundamentally change your life. I have been doing it now for 15 years, the benefits are incalculable. It's magic."

We sat in silence for the next 15 minutes. I took notes in my journal.

Len's Lessons

I make the time each day for meditation.

I am loving, forgiving, faith-full, hope-full, the light for others, joy-full, consoling, understanding, giving and self-less. I am at peace.

Prayer works. Do it every day.

Be still and know that I am God.

Give away what I want from others...first!

MY thoughts and feelings:

_____

_____

_____

_____

_____

_____

_____

_____

_____

_____

Chapter Twenty-Two

"Pessimism and Procrastination"

I was to meet Len at our favorite Starbucks. I decided to arrive an hour early, only to find him reading a copy of David Copperfield by Charles Dickens.

He smiled as I sat down. He handed me his book and said, "Read to me the section I have underlined."

Still a little frustrated by the fact that he beat me to the coffee shop, I took the book from him, put my reading glasses on and began:

Never do tomorrow what you can do today.

"Do you know anything about Mr. Micawber, the gentleman in

the story that is offering the advice?"

"No," I said, a little embarrassed. I had never read anything by Charles Dickens, though I do remember seeing "A Christmas Carol" on TV.

"Mr. Micawber was a very unsuccessful man in the story. He was offering advice that he himself had never followed. It was a warning. People, stories, illustrations come in two categories, warnings and examples. David Copperfield was being warned not to follow the same path that Mr. Micawber had."

"So, you are using a third person example in a book of fiction to teach me?"

"My secret's out," Len said with a smile. Pausing for a moment to find just the right words, he continued, "You see, Dickens was really telling us about his father. Mr. Micawber was an echo of the man his father was. He offers some additional great advice. Turn to the page I have marked with the dog-eared page..."

Finding the page corner bent back, I read aloud:

"My other piece of advice, Copperfield," Mr. Micawber said, "Annual income twenty pounds, annual expenditure nineteen pounds, six pence, result, happiness. Annual income twenty pounds, annual expenditures twenty pounds, six pence, result, misery. The blossom is blighted, the leaf withered, the God of the day goes down upon the dreary scene, and—-in short, you are forever floored. As I am!"

"What is Dickens really telling us?" Len asked with a grin.

"Well, his first warning was, don't procrastinate?"

"Yes. Now, how can you frame that in a positive opposite?"

I thought for a moment, then paraphrased, "Just do it!"

"Exactly!" Continuing on, he asked, "And the other lesson?"

"Live below your means. Spend less than you make?"

"Fascinating, isn't it? Dickens gathers up experiences from his own painful and embarrassing childhood and teaches us two simple, yet profound lessons that will change our lives and the lives of our children forever. Now do you see why I read great literature?"

"I do." I reached for my journal. I made three entries.

Just do it!

Spend less than I earn.

Both disciplines will ensure long term happiness and feelings of self worth.

Len was genuinely glad I was getting it. The lessons never stopped. He was always getting from the day, from the book, from the mistakes, not just through them.

Just then, a fellow about 35 or 40 years old, nervous, high strung, wearing a Hawaiian shirt, faded jeans, a black baseball cap, dirty sneakers, and an unkempt beard, interrupted to inject his views.

This complete stranger began, "You know, that's good advice. Most of my life I always spent more than I earned, I was always in debt, creditors chasing me day and night."

At that point, I felt resentful and turned him off. I did not hear a word he said. The uninvited and unwelcome guest rambled on for five minutes. Len listened with a kindly eye and smile. In disgust, I finally got up and bought a refill. Upon my return, he was still droning on and Len was still listening with the patience of Job. In an attempt to regain Len's time and attention, I interrupted his rude monologue.

He got the message and finally walked out with a sour look on his face.

"Can you believe that guy?"

"I can. He was a modern day Mr. Micawber. A great teacher for both you and I. He simply echoed what Dickens taught us 150 years ago. The human condition remains the same."

"But he interrupted our conversation, an uninvited guest, a party crasher!" I said with an indignant tone.

"Have you ever done that to someone?"

After a long pause, I finally admitted, "Well, I suppose I have." Gathering myself, I continued, "But I don't do that now."

"It's just where he is. He is a lonely guy, with few friends, of that I am certain. I am working today on having more compassion with the unenlightened and unaware. The Mr. Micawber's of the world are great teachers, serving as warnings."

Feeling a little ashamed, I made another note in my journal.

I want to stop being so pessimistic and judgmental. Have more patience with others, like Len.

We shook hands and Len gave me a big hug. He was a serious and committed hugger. I liked that about him. I always felt better after spending time with him.

Len's Lessons

Learn to become more tolerant.

Spend less than I earn.

Never put off to tomorrow what I might do today. Just do it!

Keep reading great books. The classic literature: Dickens, Shaw, Hemingway, Faulkner, Shakespeare, the Bible, Homer.

MY thoughts and feelings:

_____

_____

_____

_____

_____

_____

_____

_____

_____

_____

_____

Chapter Twenty-Three

"On Leaving a Legacy"

One summer day, when Len was home from college, he saw his father digging a huge hole in the back yard. Knowing his father was eighty one, and suffering from Alzheimer's disease. Len asked him what he was doing. **"I'm planting a tree,"** his father replied.

"What kind of tree is it?" Len asked with compassion and curiosity.

"It's an apple tree. Would you help me plant it?"

"Sure, Dad." Giving some thought to the idea, Len asked, "It's so small. Do you expect to live long enough to eat the apples?" As soon as he asked the question, he realized he had made a big mistake. "I'm sorry, Dad, I didn't mean…"

"Oh, that's quite all right, son, it's an honest question." Not letting his son respond, Len's Dad continued, "At my age, I know I won't. It's a small tree. It will take a few years to bear fruit."

"Then why plant it?"

"All my life I've enjoyed apples, but never from a tree I planted myself. I wouldn't have enjoyed apples all these years if other men hadn't planted trees and done what I am doing now. I'm just trying to pay the other fellows who planted apple trees before me."

That story really stuck with Len. He never forgot the lesson. Len was like that. He was a sponge. Certain lessons, he observed, had profound impacts on him. He watched what great men did and captured the lessons. In this case, the lesson was his father's selfless gift to future generations.

His father knew exactly what he was doing. His mind was clear.

Len's Lessons

What kind of trees am I planting?

What do I want to leave behind?

What will I leave my children and grandchildren?

MY thoughts and feelings:

_____

_____

_____

_____

Chapter Twenty-Four

"Judging the Judge"

"There is an old story about a Judge named Harry," Len told me one day at the coffee shop, "who lived in a posh suburb of Portland."

I leaned forward to listen intently. Len was a great storyteller.

"He was harshly criticized by his neighbors, especially the women of the area. You see, his actions and attitudes were less than positive. He was considered by most that met him to be boorish, unsociable, and curt. He rarely attended any neighborhood functions or gatherings, though his wife was always well received by the other women. The perception was she was his alter ego, enthusiastic, kind, sociable, and charming. She had the sympathy of the entire community. 'Poor dear,' the women would say. Quite sud-

denly one day, the couple moved away without a word or forwarding address. At a neighborhood barbeque the evening after their sudden departure, the women tore his reputation apart viciously like lionesses at the kill. One person sat in silence. He was a quiet young attorney who was perfectly content simply observing others.

Finally, the most outspoken of the women could stand it no longer. 'Why do you always sit silently when we talk about Harry?' she asked in an angry tone. Not pausing for an answer, she continued her tirade, 'You would think', the hostess ranted, 'from the way you've never said anything against Harry, that you approve of him?'

The young lawyer paused, composed himself and spoke. 'I'm afraid I do approve of him, certainly more than I approve of all your criticism of him over the years.' The women took umbrage to his statement. He waited for the emotional firestorm to pass, and continued.

'I learned in Law school not to form an opinion or judgment until I had all the facts. In Harry's case, it took me quite a long time to gather all the facts. Until tonight, I had no cause to share my findings. I feel compelled to tell Harry's story. This comes from another attorney friend of mine who works for a detective agency.'

The group sat in stunned silence.

'It seems the gracious wife of the Judge is a confirmed kleptomaniac. She has been caught stealing from virtually every major department store in Portland. Because of his position and influence, he was able to keep her out of jail, usually at a very heavy price. He nearly went to jail himself by drawing attention to himself and assuming the blame for the worst of her crimes. He dreaded having parties at his house because his charming wife would steal things from her guests. Furthermore, he would discourage her from attending the neighborhood gatherings because she was known to steal from other women's handbags!'

The whole group gasped in unison."

"Is that a true story?"

"Yes," Len replied. "It was this experience that taught me tolerance and being mindful of judging people. I affectionately call it 'Judging the Judge'."

I sat there for a minute contemplating the lesson. "It reminds me of the old Sioux Indian prayer," I said, paraphrasing the lesson I had learned. "Oh, Great Spirit, help me to never judge another until I have walked two weeks in his moccasins."

"By Jove, I think you've got it!" Len said in a bad English accent.

Len's Lessons

Judge not lest ye be judged.

Walk a mile in the other person's shoes first.

You never know what someone else is going through. Keep opinions of others to yourself until you have all the facts.

Some people are really good actors. You just never know.

MY thoughts and feelings:

_____

_____

_____

Chapter Twenty-Five

HONE$TY

"Honesty Habit"

I came to Len one day for a confession. I had lied to my boss at work. He knew I had and confronted me. I admitted it and we moved on, but he gave me a stern warning. "That's the one and only time, Steve. If you lie to me again, I will let you go."

Len just listened, then he gave me that look. He leaned forward.

"Do you know who we tell the first lie to?"

I shook my head, no.

"Ourselves." Earl Nightingale said years ago, "If honesty didn't exist, someone would surely invent it as the fastest way to become wealthy."

Len paused for effect.

"Shakespeare said, 'To thine own self be true.' It starts when we are very young. When Daniel was about five, he was very interested in hockey. One morning on my way out to work, I saw 10 tennis balls lined up about ten feet from the dryer in the garage and a hockey stick holding them in place. My wife had told me not to disturb them, as he was going to 'practice' today hitting shots into the open dryer!"

He smiled as he continued.

"I came home that night and there was a cold blast hitting me in the face when I stepped out of the car. The source? It was a broken window with a hole about as big as a tennis ball would make. I called Daniel into the garage. He had a look of fear like I had never seen."

"I knelt down to his eye level and asked, 'What happened to the window, buddy?' He broke down and started crying as he explained the errant shot off the dryer. I smiled and said, 'It must have been hard for you to tell me the truth. I'm so proud of you.'"

'You're not going to spank me?'

'No, son, I am so glad you told me the truth.' I gave him a big hug.

"Wow. You were rewarding honesty!"

"Yes. Do you know, to this day, Daniel is the most honest person I know. He is a terrible liar."

I was pondering the lessons in his story.

"Why do we lie?"

"Many reasons, the big one is fear. Fear of losing something we have or afraid of not getting something we want."

"Is that it?"

"No, in my experience it goes much deeper. It's a form of control."

"Manipulation?"

"Absolutely. It's avoiding personal responsibility, a selfish way of getting out of being accountable for our own behavior."

"So, when we start telling the truth, it's a way of growing up?"

"Very much so. You see, if we tell the truth, we don't have to remember what we said."

"Whoa, I have been working waaay too hard!"

Len burst out laughing. He threw his head back. In the time I had known Len, he had only done that a few other times. I had hit the nail on the head.

"Big people admit they make mistakes. That's probably why your boss gave you a second chance. He knows we all make mistakes. Honesty is a habit."

I leaned forward and said, "One that is hard to form, but easy to live with?"

"By Jove, I think he's got it, Watson! It's the end of blame and the beginning of growing up."

Now it was my turn to quote Shakespeare, "Oh, what a tangled web we weave, when first we practice to deceive."
Len smiled and touched me on the shoulder.

"We need to examine our past, our motives and intent. Although the truth is painful at times, the alternative is always ten times worse."

I had much to ponder that night. I filled up my journal.

Len's Lessons

If I tell the truth, I don't have to remember what I said.

To thine own self be true.

Big people admit when they are wrong.

Honesty is a good habit that's hard to form, but easy to live with.

Reward honesty or any other behavior I want those around me to embrace.

MY thoughts and feelings:

_____

_____

_____

_____

_____

_____

_____

Chapter Twenty-Six

"Maxims for the Mind"

Proverbs, maxims and aphorisms have a way of sticking to us as maple syrup to a five-year old's hands at a pancake breakfast. It began when Len's father shared his with Len in the form of a letter. From that point forward, Len collected them like kids collect baseball cards. He captured them in his journal as they happened, or as they happened upon him.

Len's father said to him that night of the wedding, "Son, to get the most from this information, read and reread these quotes. Burn them into your memory. They will become part of your life and enrich your journey.

They certainly represent some of the best ideas from Len's journals. They are truly his last lessons.

After I read them, I wrote my favorite ones in my journal and then began the marvelous journey of collecting my own. What a wonderful shade tree for my children's children. Imagine, long after I'm gone to the sweet hereafter, my family and friends will discover these gems, like buried treasure.

I want my journey of discovery and wonder to include my own lessons and aphorisms in my own hand, written with love like a time capsule for future generations. It will be more valuable than my house or savings account.

Life is a series of lessons, both positive and negative. Len would have you enjoy them all...a day at a time.

The last thing Len wanted to leave with me was the following simple process:

"Have you ever been blue, despondent, full of fear?" he asked one day when it was clear he was reading my mind.

"Of course," I said. I leaned in to listen.

Here is a simple formula that has helped me many times pull out of the doldrums, the blues, self pity. He handed me a piece of paper:

The next time you're blue, frustrated, down, and we all feel that way from time to time, read and practice this for one week, 7-days. It works like magic:

1. Get up at 0600 no matter what time you went to bed the night before and go for a brisk 2-3 mile walk.

2. Shower, change into a nice outfit, ironed, pressed and clean. Dress for work even if you work at home.

3. Read something inspirational for 20-30 minutes. Choose from

the Bible, an inspiring Biography or autobiography or classic self-help book. A classic is one that has stood the test of time and continues to sell well 20, 30, 60 years after it was first printed.

4. Plan your day. List the six most important things and prioritize. Then do the first item on your list.

5. Go out into the world with a different attitude. Smile, throw your shoulders back, sit up straight and greet people with enthusiasm, eye contact and a firm handshake. Let them know you are genuinely glad to see them.

6. Offer up a word of encouragement, a kind gesture. People are starving for acknowledgment and recognition. Observe the obvious and comment on it. "Those are great shoes," or "How long did it take to get that kind of shine on that car?" You get the idea. Something they are obviously proud of.

7. Learn at least three funny, clean stories and tell them with regularity. Silly is fine, short is fine.

8. Ask people about their interests and passions and dominate the listening. Everyone has a story. Your job is to find out what that is.

9. Find someone to help. Pay attention, the opportunity is everywhere.

10. Pray and listen. Prayer is talking to God, meditation is listening to God. Pause throughout the day to breathe, give thanks and listen.

11. Do something you are afraid of doing every day. Take a chance, a risk, face your fears and act. Stretch your comfort zones.

12. Keep what you do for others a secret. Write it in your journal, but keep quiet about it.

That's it. If you do these 12 things when you are down, I promise, you will not feel the same when you are done.

When I asked Len where all this information came from, he told me a story. He said it summarized how he felt for all the gifts he received from others over the years.

There was this fellow with an ugly dog. He kept taking the dog to dog shows around the country year after year. Finally, his best friend pulled him aside and said, "Look, I care about you, you're my best friend. Why do you insist on taking that mutt of yours to shows year after year? He is so ugly; he will never win a prize. Everyone wants to know, why?" After some thought and reflection, the fellow replied, "You're right, he is ugly and I am aware he will never win a prize. The reason I continue traveling around the country is simple...look at all the great dogs he has had the privilege to hang around the last ten years!"

We hugged.

He smiled and waved as he drove away.

That was the last time I ever saw him alive.

I miss him every day.

Notes

Notes

Mark Matteson is President of Pinnacle Service Group.

Mark is the author of the best selling book "Freedom From Fear."

Whether it's to a small company of 50 people or to an international audience of 2,500, he is in great demand Internationally as a Keynote Speaker, Seminar Leader and Management Consultant on such topics as:

* Sales Achievement
* Customer Service Excellence
* Attracting, Hiring and Retaining Employees
* "Freedom From Fear"(The Seminar)
* Developing Vision, Values, Goals
* Presenting Like a Pro
* Front Line Sales

Mark has developed an international reputation for his Humorous, Unique and Profit Producing seminars and Keynote Presentations. Mark inspires Fortune 500 Companies, Manufacturers,

Distributors, Associations and Service Organizations Nationwide to "Raise the Bar" to achieve higher levels of personal and professional performance.

To contact Mark for Keynote presentations, Seminars or Consulting or to receive your FREE e-zine each month, go to www.MattesonAvenue.com

Pinnacle Service Group
Raising the Bar in Organizations Nationwide
Telephone Toll Free 877.672.2001
Fax 425.745.8981
mark@mattesonavenue.com
www.mattesonavenue.com

Order Form

Fax, mail or order securely on-line the following products:

qty	item	each	total
____	Freedom From Fear (book)	9.99	_____
____	Freedom From Fear Forever	14.95	_____
____	FFF audio CD	29.95	_____
____	FFFF audio CD	39.95	_____
____	FFF Window Cards	9.95	_____
____	FFFF the Journal	14.95	_____
____	4-color journal pen	3.95	_____
	Shipping ($4.95 for up to 3 items)............		_____
	Total..		_____

www.mattesonavenue.com

Fax to 425-745-8981

Mail to:
Pinnacle Service Group
6722 163rd Place SW
Lynnwood, WA 98037

Visit www.ffffbook.com for updates and tools for growth

Order Form

Fax, mail or order securely on-line the following products:

qty	item	each	total
___	Freedom From Fear (book)	9.99	_____
___	Freedom From Fear Forever	14.95	_____
___	FFF audio CD	29.95	_____
___	FFFF audio CD	39.95	_____
___	FFF Window Cards	9.95	_____
___	FFFF the Journal	14.95	_____
___	4-color journal pen	3.95	_____
	Shipping ($4.95 for up to 3 items).............		_____
	Total..		_____

www.mattesonavenue.com

Fax to 425-745-8981

Mail to:
Pinnacle Service Group
6722 163rd Place SW
Lynnwood, WA 98037

Visit www.ffffbook.com for updates and tools for growth

Contact:

Mark Matteson
mark@mattesonavenue.com

Kevin Thomas
kevin@mattesonavenue.com

David Harrison
davidh@mattesonavenue.com

David Marty
davidm@mattesonavenue.com

or visit www.mattesonavenue.com and follow the links.

Freedom From Fear Forever supplies tremendous inspiration. No matter your background, desires, or description of success, this book provides direction through insightful stories and teachings that reach a true level of understanding. A cut above, Freedom From Fear Forever drives home a recipe for action and lays the foundation for success in family, business, leadership, and in life.

> Major Guy J. Brilando
> ASAFR - 56th Training Squadron - Luke AFB

Freedom from Fear Forever serves as a great reminder to all of us that execution is what really counts. All the best ideas and best intentions will fall flat without a concerted effort toward implementation. This book will help thousands of people to reach their goals.

> Mike Murphy
> Business Editor - The News Magazine

Better than the original. Mark's work truly makes you sit back and contemplate what your priorities in life are, and what they should be. *Freedom From Fear Forever* is a "must read" for family, friends, and work associates because it focuses on how you should change your mindset every day, and your life will change. Mark's message is that it is not just about having a positive attitude, it's about making changes in your daily activities, and watch the results come to you. It's about taking action in addition to attitude!!

> Matt Peterson
> Vice President – Sales and Marketing - York International

www.fffbook.com